INVESTING IN

PENSIONS

Copyright © Templar Publishing Ltd 1988

First published in Great Britain in 1988
by Ward Lock Limited, 8 Clifford Street, London W1X 1RB
An Egmont Company

All rights reserved.
No part of this publication may be reproduced, stored in a
retrieval system, or transmitted, in any form or by any
means, electronic, mechanical, photocopying, recording,
or otherwise, without the prior permission of the
copyright holder and publisher.

The publisher and copyright holder wish to point out that
any names and addresses used as examples within this
book are fictitious, and are not intended to represent
existing companies or individuals.

Designed and produced by Templar Publishing Ltd
107 High Street, Dorking, Surrey RH4 1QA
Typeset by Templar Type
Printed and bound in Great Britain
by Richard Clay Ltd
Chichester, Sussex

British Library Cataloguing in Publication Data

Spill, Ron
Investing in Pensions.—(You and your money series)
1. Old age pensions—Great Britain
2. Penion trusts—Great Britain
I. Title   II. Series
331.25'2'0941   HD7105.35.G7

ISBN 0-7063-6646-8

INVESTING IN

PENSIONS

RON SPILL

Ward Lock · London

CONTENTS

Examples included in this book are based on the tax position current for the financial year 1987 - 1988. Budgets often concern themselves with pensions and nearly always affect rates of income tax, so any changes to these examples brought about by the 1988 Budget need to be taken into account by the reader.

INTRODUCTION

If you compare a few of the retired people you know, it is obvious that their life styles vary a great deal. The differences can't always be explained entirely by the amount of money they had in the days when they were working, or by the kind of money they are receiving now. But generally speaking, a retired person's or a couple's ability to do much better than merely make ends meet has a lot to do with the planning which went into organising their retirement income years ago.

It is not necessarily any planning they did of their own deliberate choice. They paid their National Insurance contributions without any option. And, if they were lucky enough to be in a pension scheme run by the firm they worked for, this was usually because joining the scheme was a condition of the job.

In many cases, however, they were given the opportunity to invest quite voluntarily for the kind of retirement income they'd like to live on. Some grasped the opportunity, even though doing so made a noticeable hole in their take-home pay. Others, probably the majority, turned it down. Usually this was a decision which a married man, often the only or the main bread-winner, took by himself. But the result was not just financial disadvantage for him in his retired years, it would be a disadvantage too for his wife if she became a widow. Sadly, because wives are usually a few years younger than their husbands and statistically can be expected to live longer than men of the same age, widows are the poorest section of the long term poor in the population.

The purpose of a pension is to maintain a standard of living into retirement which is not very different from what it was in the few years before retirement. For most people, with the house paid for and the children grown up and flown the nest, those years in the run-up to retirement are a period of comparative affluence. This book aims to show what your chances are of building up the decent pension you want for yourself and for your wife or husband. And how, if the chances don't look altogether bright, you can make the most of the options which periodically come your way, especially the option of paying extra contributions with the unfailing assistance of the taxman, whose generosity has been regularly confirmed by successive governments' tax laws.

This book has another purpose too: to simplify and demystify the complex and often mysterious world of pensions.

· 1 ·

WHERE PENSIONS COME FROM

As things stand, you can expect your regular retirement income to come from four main sources: the State; your present and maybe your previous jobs; your own initiative in taking out your own pension plan; and savings you have as a result of other kinds of investment or, say, of moving to a less expensive house when you retire, pocketing the profit. This chapter is about the first three of these sources and takes each in turn.

STATE PENSIONS

Everyone with a paid job bringing in more than £41 a week (1988-89 figure) pays National Insurance contributions and, apart from some married women and widows who chose years ago to contribute at a special reduced rate, each wage earner is entitled to the basic flat-rate State pension. For the year April 1988 to April 1989 this pension stands at £41.15 a week for a single person. For a married couple where the wife has not made full National Insurance contributions from her own earnings, the rate is £65.90 a week. To these rates a small supplement is added for people who paid 'graduated contributions' between 1961 and 1975, but it won't amount to much.

Traditionally, State pensions go up each year to keep their purchasing power more or less intact. The basic pension goes up each April in line with the increase in retail prices over the 12 months up to the previous September. The amount of the increase is announced in the newspapers each October. But the basic pension does not go up in line with the increases in average earnings, although it used to whenever these outstripped price increases. As a result, the basic pension for a single person is now about 20 per cent of the national average wage, or about 33 per cent for a married couple.

In time, this percentage will fall if earnings continue to outstrip prices. So, on the present basis, by the year 2018 the percentages you receive may be only 10 per cent and 16 per cent of average earnings. (A special treat lies in wait for you if you reach 80 years of age: the pension goes up suddenly by 25p!)

Fortunately, there's another State pension too. This is SERPS, the State earnings-related pension scheme which, after years of party-political wrangling about the State's role in organising pensions, was introduced in 1978 with support from both Labour and Conservative parties. The original SERPS aim was to give you an extra 25 per cent of at least part of your earnings. For example, if you earn £241 a week, disregard the first £41 a week. The SERPS pension formula was 25 per cent of the remaining £200 a week, so giving you a pension of £50 a week. If you earn more than £305 a week you have to disregard anything above that level. And if you reach the official starting date for receiving a State pension – 65 for men and 60 for women – before April 1998, the 25 per cent pension will be scaled down. These figures are the ones for the year April 1988 to April 1989 and every year they go up in line with increases in average earnings. However, the way SERPS pensions are worked out is being changed. Chapter 5 has the details, but keeping with the example, the SERPS pension of £50 a week is likely to be cut to £40 and probably less if you reach State pension age after the year 2010.

The conclusion you ought to draw from this brief description of State pensions is that they are not enough to live on comfortably. The table below shows this very clearly. For someone on average earnings retiring in 1978, just as SERPS was starting, the pension was about 23 per cent of earnings. For someone retiring in 1988, it's about 30 per cent. And it reaches a peak for someone retiring in 1998 of nearly 40 per cent. But then it begins to fall away, so that for someone retiring in 2018 the total State pension will be back to about the same 23 per cent of earnings that it was in 1978.

STATE PENSION AS % OF AVERAGE EARNINGS

The table shows how the State pensions will provide a smaller percentage of average earnings after the end of the century. (Assumes basic pension is linked to RPI and increases at 5% p.a., and Average earnings increase at 7% p.a.)

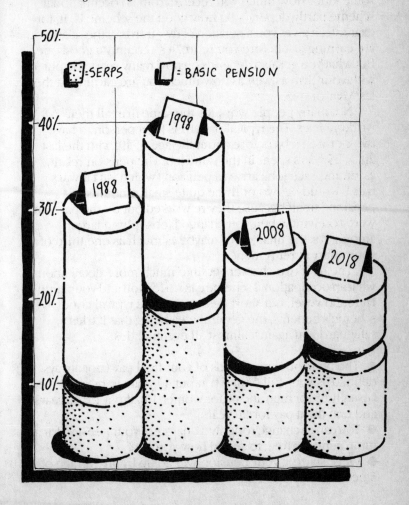

OCCUPATIONAL PENSIONS

These are pensions which come with the job you do, if you are one of the 11 million people – that's about half the working population – whose employers sponsor a pension scheme of some kind. How much you receive from an occupational scheme partly depends on how good the scheme is. If, for example, it gives you a pension of two-thirds of the salary you are earning just before you retire, it's certainly a good one. But what you get also depends on how many years you put in with your firm as well as how much you are earning in the last year or two.

Not many people work for the same firm all their working lives. The typical pattern is for a person to have two or three jobs before about the age of 40, with the last 20 or 25 years spent in the same job. The pension result, assuming each job carries a pension (which isn't always true), would be two or three quite small amounts of pension (small because they're worked out on the pay you were receiving when you changed jobs) plus a larger amount for the final job of maybe as much as one-third of your salary at retirement.

The next two chapters go into much more detail about what an occupational scheme can do for you and your family. Here, however, is a short description of a typical good scheme's benefits, the general idea being that it tries to safeguard you against almost all eventualities:

● The pension is two-thirds of your final pay (not always defined as your full pay) if you put 40 years in by retirement (usually 65 for men and 60 for women), half-pay for 30 years and one-third pay for 20 years.
● You can exchange roughly a quarter of your pension for a lump sum, tax free, to spend how you like.
● Once started, your pension will go up by an average of 5 per cent a year to help with rising prices.

● If your wife (or possibly, if you are a woman, your husband) outlives you, she will receive half your pension for the rest of her life.

● If you die before retirement, your family will receive two years' pay tax free, with a widow's (sometimes a widower's) pension for life of half the pension you would have received at retirement.

● If ill health forces you to retire early, you are entitled to an immediate pension based on the years you have put in so far, plus half that for the years you won't be putting in between now and your normal retirement date.

● If after at least two years in the scheme you change jobs, you may leave behind the pension rights you have built up so far and draw them when you finally retire. Or you can transfer them to your next employer's scheme or to a pension plan of your own.

● You contribute 5 per cent of your earnings and your employer pays the rest of the required cost.

INDIVIDUAL PENSIONS

For many years the self-employed (about three million people) and those who work for a firm which does not run an occupational pension scheme have had the right to receive the same kind of tax relief on contribution to a personal pension plan as those in occupational schemes. In fact, it has only been the self-employed who have taken out such plans in large numbers, partly because, unlike employees, they do not qualify for SERPS pensions.

Not all self-employed people, however, adopt these plans and many who do will not receive adequate pensions because they have not committed themselves to investing enough. The law on personal pension plans has been changed in order to encourage more people to invest in these plans and this subject is dealt with in more detail in later chapters.

To give an idea of how a fairly typical personal pension works, let us suppose a man retiring this year at 65 has built up an investment of £100,000. He takes the maximum possible tax free cash sum of £25,000 plus a pension of £6,600 a year. This method of building up retirement benefits is quite different from the way in which occupational pension schemes work. The occupational scheme starts with the benefits you are to get, leaving you and your firm to contribute whatever is necessary to pay for them. But the personal pension starts from the contributions you pay. Then, the amount of capital these have accumulated after being invested over the years to retirement is used to buy you a pension at the rates current at the time. (You may come across the jargon used to describe this approach – it's known as the 'money purchase' or 'defined contributions' method.)

Contrasting the benefits of occupations pensions with those available from personal pensions is not very relevant if you're self-employed or your firm doesn't run an occupational pension for you. However, to summarise the differences is useful: an occupational scheme will give you excellent benefits if you don't have many job changes. On the other hand, a personal pension isn't affected by job changes – you take it with you. It's under your personal control and, provided you accept that you must regularly re-appraise the level of contributions you're putting in, it can give you the retirement benefits you need.

PENSIONS AND POLITICS

Ever since the 1950s, one government after another has tried to reshape the ways in which people can provide for their retirement. Very broadly, Labour has favoured a framework in which adequate State pensions are available to those whose jobs do not carry a good pension. By contrast, the Conservatives have come to favour a system in which there is a place for a very basic State pension, but with the bulk of

· PERSONAL PENSION ·

① You decide on your monthly contributions.

② On retirement, you have built up a 'Pension' fund.

③ You use this fund to 'buy' a pension.

· OCCUPATIONAL PENSION ·

① Your company pays a percentage of your salary into the pension scheme on your behalf (you usually have to make a contribution too).

② Each year's contribution earns you e.g. $\frac{1}{60}$ of your salary as a retirement pension.

③ When you retire you will receive a pension of up to e.g. $\frac{40}{60}$ of your final salary.

15

pension provision coming either from the firm an employee works for or from his/her own resources.

Both Labour and Conservative governments have been in broad agreement over the need to make all pension contributions attractive from the point of view of tax relief. And because of the helpful system of tax concessions now in force, successive governments have felt justified in ensuring that all private pensions meet certain minimum standards of adequacy, but do not exceed certain maximum levels by which they would exploit the tax relief system.

Two government agencies have this supervisory role: the Occupational Pensions Board, which reports to the Department of Health and Social Security, sees to it that standards are adequate, while the Superannuation Funds Office, which is part of the Inland Revenue, ensures that the system of tax relief is not exploited.

TRADE UNION VIEWS

Before the 1970s, the trade union opinion about pensions was broadly that people should be able to look forward to an adequate pension from a perfected State pension system. However, in the mid-1970s it became clear to them that there was no good reason why large numbers of manual workers should not expect as good an occupational pensions deal from their firms as their white-collar colleagues. While not backing away from their belief in State pension provision, trade unions soon began to put occupational pensions for all employees high on their list of objectives in their negotiations.

Since the early 1980s, the modern trade unions have aimed to provide a wide range of financial services to their members, with pensions ranking as a very most important item. So, wherever it is officially recognised, a trade union sees itself as having a vital role in being responsible for negotiating improvements to occupational pension schemes.

But, more than that, some unions have also come to see themselves as the agency through which individual plans can be organised for people whose employers do not run a pension scheme which includes them.

THE PENSIONS INDUSTRY

With more than twelve million people contributing to some kind of occupational or personal pension plan, it's not surprising that the business of supplying pensions these days has become a major industry investing very large sums – the total contribution recently being paid in was some £12 billion. The only contact you have yourself with this industry may be the pensions officer where you work or the insurance company representative who fixed you up with a personal pension plan.

The main components of the pensions business are:

● **The pension funds.** These are the large employer-sponsored pension schemes which for many years have had their own association to protect their interests. Typically, a big pension fund is managed by a pensions manager and his department, who are responsible for maintaining records, collecting contributions from the employers, paying benefits out as they fall due and, most important, investing the contributions to the best effect.

● **Insurance companies.** These are the specialist companies that look after pension funds on behalf of many employers' schemes as well as those of individual holders. These companies also provide insurance cover to the occupational pension scheme so that benefits can be paid out on an employee's death before retirement. (In fact the larger pension funds often do not insure this risk.) Unit trust companies now also manage pension schemes.

● **Investment managers.** These include banks, the investment departments of insurance companies and, in the case of some of the largest pension schemes, a directly employed investment team. These people are hired to manage the investments wisely and successfully within the various chosen investment sectors, such as UK and overseas shares, government securities, property and cash deposits.

● **Consulting actuaries and pensions consultants.** The main responsibility of actuaries and consultants is to advise those who run pension schemes about the level of contributions needed to pay for the promised benefits, and to ensure that the scheme's assets and liabilities are kept in reasonable equilibrium. They also advise on the benefits themselves, frequently in response to the demands of the latest pension or tax regulations.

● **Insurance consultants.** These people mainly advise employers about their pension schemes, but they will also advise individual members of the public about personal pensions.

There are many other professional people involved in pensions too, such as auditors, who vet an occupational pension scheme's accounts, and solicitors, who are responsible for the legal work in setting up new schemes and amending existing ones. And there are communications experts who advise on video programmes, booklets, broadsheets and all the other items needed to explain a pension scheme to its members.

· 2 ·

OCCUPATIONAL PENSION SCHEMES
Their benefits

When you start working for a new firm, the first thing you
may be told about the company pension scheme is that you
will be eligible to join it in six months' time and that as a
condition of employment you will have to contribute to it.
This compulsion has now disappeared. Eventually, you are
given an explanatory booklet with details of the benefits and
options you can expect for yourself and your family. You may
even be invited to a film show which highlights the scheme's
main attractions.

Behind all this is a complex legal and financial
apparatus which may have been started many years ago,
when your firm set up a 'trust' fund to collect and invest the
contributions from the firm and its employees. By law this
trust fund must be quite separate from the firm's business.
This means that if the firm fails at some time, the
employees' pension rights don't disappear with it. The trust
fund is administered by a number of legally appointed
trustees, usually no less than three and no more than six. The
firm's senior executives often act as trustees, but
sometimes one or more employee representatives are
appointed. In large firms where trade unions have
negotiating rights, employee representatives may number as
many as half of the trustees.

The job of the trustees is to see that the contributions
arrive on time, are invested in the pension scheme
members' best interests and finally produce the benefits
which the scheme has promised. As an individual you have
the legal right to see the documents which set out the
trustees' duties and the members' rights and options in
complete detail. These are called the trust deed and rules.

Because they are meant to stand up in a court of law and need to fulfil complex legal and tax requirements, they are usually, however, impenetrable to the layman.

Most employees rely on the explanatory booklet to see what benefits they can expect. As a rough guide to the benefits here is a brief example based on a member of a 'final salary' scheme. (Another type, known as 'money purchase' is described later in this chapter.)

> John Brown joins ABC Limited when he is 24. A year later, at 25, he is eligible for the pension scheme and, if he joins, is required to contribute as a condition of employment 5 per cent of his basic earnings on which he receives tax relief. The firm's contribution changes from time to time but is usually around 10 per cent of the total basic earnings of all the scheme members.

THE PENSION

John is promised a pension of one-sixtieth of his final pensionable earnings for each year he works for ABC Limited from the age of 25 to retirement age. (Retirement age is set at 65 for men, 60 for women.) His 'final pensionable earnings' are defined as the average of his best three consecutive years' basic earnings in the last ten years before retirement. These will probably be his last three years, so his pension will be 40-sixtieths, or two-thirds, of his average final pay.

He is contracted out of SERPS, the State earnings-related pension scheme, so his National Insurance contribution is at the lower rate. As a result he will only collect the basic flat-rate State pension because the ABC Limited scheme must pay him a pension as good as the SERPS pension. In fact it will be much better.

When he begins to draw his pension, his State pension and his ABC Limited pension are added together for tax purposes. He has to pay PAYE tax just as he did when he was earning, but all the tax is deducted from his ABC Limited pension, not his State pension. So when the State pension goes up, he has to pay a bit more tax out of his ABC Limited pension.

The choice – pension or cash?

Shortly before he retires he will be given a choice between taking his pension in full or taking a reduced amount plus a lump sum of one-and-a-half times his final pensionable earnings. If these earnings were £12,000 a year and his full pension were £8,000 a year, his alternative reduced pension would be £6,000 a year and his lump sum would be £18,000. This sum would be tax-free. (The equivalent figures for a woman retiring at 60 are different. Assuming the same earnings and full pension rights her reduced pension would be £6,364, though the lump sum would still be £18,000.)

Pension increases

When John retires the first monthly instalment of his pension should reach him the following day. On each anniversary of his retirement he will receive an increase in his pension of a guaranteed 3 per cent plus, every two or three years, an extra increase if the scheme's investments have performed well or if the firm has made good profits. The part of his pension he would have drawn from SERPS if he had not been contracted-out is also uprated annually in line with the cost of living index, partly by ABC Limited, partly by the DHSS.

Death benefits

If John dies within five years of retiring, his dependants will be given a tax-free lump sum. This lump sum is equal to the pension he would have been paid over the rest of the five years.

If he dies leaving a widow, she will be paid for life a pension of half what he was drawing – or would have been drawing if he had not taken part of his pension as a lump sum.

Up to retirement John was covered for two kinds of death benefit. The first was a lump sum of two years' earnings paid tax-free to his dependants. The second was a widow's pension, paid for life, of half the pension he could have expected at 65 based on his current pensionable earnings. (If the narrative had been about a woman, there would probably have been little or no mention of a widower's pension, regardless of when her death took place.)

Early retirement

If John retired early for one of three reasons he could have taken his pension straight away. First, he could have been forced into it by ill health. In that case, the £8,000 a year pension he was expecting at 65 would have been paid immediately without any reduction.

Second, he could have been made redundant with the offer of an immediate pension. If this had happened when he still had six years to go to normal retirement at 65, the immediate pension might have been based on the 34 years he had actually worked plus half of the six years he wouldn't be working. This 37 years would have given him a pension of £7,400 a year.

The third possibility is that he could have given up work voluntarily. In this case retiring six years early would have given him an immediate pension of £4,350 a year because it would have been based only on the 34 years he had actually worked and then been reduced because it was going to be paid for six years longer than normal.

Extra contributions

At any time during his membership of the scheme John could have paid extra contributions to boost his own pension. He might have seen little sense in that because the scheme seemed to him quite adequate. But if he had ever been worried about being retired on a reduced pension at, say, 60, or if he had earned a lot more than just the basic earnings on which the scheme calculates the pension, he might have acted differently. If he had joined the scheme at 35 or 40 instead of at 25, and was therefore unable to qualify for a full 40-year pension, this option would have enabled him substantially to improve his ultimate pension and pension rights.

Changing jobs

If John had left the company to go to another job after being in the scheme for two years or more, he would have had two options. He could either have left behind the pension rights built up so far for collection when he eventually retired. Alternatively, he could have transferred the cash value to the scheme run by his new firm, or to a pension plan in his own name.

This example displays some key features which could make all the difference as to how good a pension you retire on and how well your family is protected if you die prematurely. Understanding these key features will help you to judge how good your firm's pension scheme is. They are:

THE PENSION FRACTION

Most schemes give you a pension of one-sixtieth of your earnings for each year worked. Some will give a better fraction, such as one-forty-fifth, and some a worse fraction, such as one-eightieth. Schemes run by employers in the public sector – the Civil Service and local government for example –

nearly always give one-eightieth. This produces a pension of half pay for a 40-year career, but there is always an automatic tax-free lump sum which is three times the annual pension.

HOW EARNINGS ARE DEFINED
Fraction sizes are important, but the earnings they are applied to are equally important. Some earnings definitions leave out everything you earn on top of your basic pay, like commission and bonuses, and reduce it by some figure to allow for the basic State pension, maybe £2,000 or £3,000 a year. Also, some schemes work your pension out on your pay in your last year at work while others take a three-year average. This could be less favourable to you unless your earnings fell away in your final couple of years at work.

PENSION INCREASES
Even when inflation pushes up prices quite slowly, you still need protection against it. Public sector schemes nearly always automatically increase pensions in line with prices. Some schemes in the private sector however, never increase your pension, and some only guarantee to increase it each year by 3 per cent or 5 per cent, or only if there is a surplus in the fund, or if the firm's profits permit. This can mean that sometimes you will get a bigger increase than the rise in retail price index, sometimes less. Some schemes which rely on this discretionary approach have a deliberate policy of always matching a proportion (75 per cent, for instance) of the increase in the retail price index (RPI).

DEATH BENEFITS
Sometimes the pension paid to a widow or widower is a little larger, and occasionally a lot less, than the half-rate pension in the John Brown example. And the lump sum of two years' pay can be as much as four years' pay, but it may be a lot less too.

You may find quaint rules like the one which decrees that a widow's pension stops or is cut back if she remarries. It is always worth checking the small print in your firm's scheme to establish exactly what your family can expect. You can find out more about this in Chapter 8 which explains pensions for women.

EARLY RETIREMENT

There is a wide variety of ways in which this is treated. In the example, John Brown would, in fact have been treated rather well, whatever the reason for retiring early – ill health, redundancy or voluntary retirement. But some schemes treat retirement on the grounds of ill health and redundancy as if these were voluntary decisions. At least, that is how the explanatory booklet may put it. In the event, you may achieve a better pension because your firm decides to contribute extra for you.

When you look at your own firm's scheme, you may be disappointed with the way it tackles some of these key features. It is worth remembering, however, that pension schemes have not all been improved in the same areas at the same time. Fortunately for you, making improvements every few years is a regular activity for a great many pension schemes and in any case you should really judge the scheme you belong to or are thinking of joining, as a complete package to which your firm may contribute twice as much as you do.

MONEY PURCHASE SCHEMES

Most employees in occupational pension schemes are destined for the kind of 'final salary' pension described in the John Brown example. But there are many employees, particularly those working in smaller firms, whose pensions are organised on 'money purchase' lines. On the next page there is another example, from which you will see that a typical 'money purchase' scheme is much simpler.

Henry Green works for the XYZ Company Limited and has been contributing 4 per cent of his basic pay into its pension scheme since he was 35. He gets tax relief on his contributions. His firm pays another 4 per cent and the joint contribution of 8 per cent is invested.

When he reaches retirement age (65 for him but 60 for women), his pension will be based on the amount of invested contributions standing in his own 'personal account'.

Like John Brown, he too plans to take as much as possible as a tax-free lump sum. In his case, it would be the equivalent of just over a year's pay. The balance in his 'personal account' is used to buy him a pension for life. Strictly speaking, he will buy what is called an 'annuity'. He has the option of arranging it so that it increases each year. Since he is married he plans to arrange for half his pension to continue to be paid to his wife if he is the first to die. Putting this into figures, if he is earning £12,000 a year just before he retires and his account then stands at £50,000, his lump sum would be £13,500. The remaining £36,500 in his account would buy him a pension of £4,000 a year, and his wife a widow's pension of £2,000 a year should her husband die first.

If he dies before retirement, the invested contributions will be paid tax free to his family along with one year's pay, also tax free, which the firm has paid for.

If he changes jobs having completed two years or more in the scheme, he can leave his account behind to grow until he retires, or he can transfer it to his next employer's scheme or to a pension plan of his own choosing.

He is not contracted out of SERPS, the State earnings-related pension scheme, so he will receive in addition both the basic State pension and the SERPS pension when he retires. If, on the other hand, his firm decide to contract-out, he would forego any further build-up of his SERPS pension. He would, however, pay lower National Insurance contributions, and invest what he saves (about 2 per cent of his earnings) to boost his pension from the firm's scheme.

Generally, someone who stays with the same firm for the whole of his working life will do better with 'final salary' than with 'money purchase' schemes. This comparison is, however, fairly meaningless. People do change jobs quite frequently and in any case they are not usually offered a choice of schemes by their firms.

For most people the best option is to sign up for a scheme as soon as it's offered to you. If the benefits of the scheme do not look like being adequate, then you should consider paying extra contributions, or setting up a scheme of your own.

PUBLIC SECTOR SCHEMES

This chapter has mostly been about schemes run by firms in the private sector. Schemes in the public sector (such as civil and local government service and nationalised industries) resemble 'final salary' schemes quite closely, though there are three main differences:

The first is that they place more emphasis on a regular income than on a cash lump sum when it comes to benefits for your family if you die before retirement.

The second is that the retirement benefit is expressed not as a pension of which part can be taken as tax-free cash, but simply as a pension plus a tax-free cash sum. The formula is usually one-eightieth of final earnings for each qualifying year worked as the pension and three-eightieths for each such year as the cash. For a 40-year career this means a half-pay pension and 18 months' pay in cash.

The third difference is that public sector pensions are linked to the retail price index; that is, they usually maintain their purchasing power, something which private sector schemes would like, but cannot always afford, to do.

· 3 ·

OCCUPATIONAL PENSION SCHEMES
What regulates them and how they are paid

For an occupational pension scheme to win the blessing of the tax authorities, the firm must contribute to it. In the case of money purchase schemes it's usually a simple matter of the firm deciding what it wants to pay and whether it wants to put in more for some employees than for others.

But in the case of a final salary scheme, what the firm contributes is rather more complicated. The scheme is promising to pay you and your colleagues a pension based on your earnings at a retirement date which could be more than 40 years away. During that time earnings will rise, investment conditions will change, the average age of the members may alter, employees will change jobs and, though life expectancy in general may improve, a few of them will die. So how, when the future is full of so many unknowns, can anyone say what money should be invested to make sure that the pension promises are kept? The answer is that, although no one can predict the future with complete accuracy, well-educated predictions which are regularly monitored can and do produce contribution levels which usually stay remarkably stable over long periods of time.

This prediction business is a job for the experts. These experts are called actuaries. Every final salary scheme, whether it's a multi-million pound affair covering thousands of employees or a 30-employee scheme with £100,000 of assets, has got an actuary in the background. His job is to set out a series of assumptions of which the two most important are the future rate of pay increases and future investment returns. He then has to work out what percentage of the total payroll of scheme members needs to be invested each year if the pension promises are to be met. In effect, he has to ensure that the present and future commitments of the scheme are adequately backed by its investments.

He might put it like this: suppose the scheme were to be closed down in five years, is there enough money invested to cover the pension rights which the employees will have accumulated by then? His conclusion might be that the contribution rate needs to be 12 per cent of the pensionable payroll. This would mean that the firm should pay 7 per cent on top of the 5 per cent contributed by the scheme members. This kind of assessment takes place every three years or so. The actuary looks at the schemes, investments and commitments and produces a 'valuation report'. If his assumptions have been more or less borne out by what has happened, and still look reasonable for the next few years, he would probably recommend that the same contribution level should be maintained. But if something unusual has happened, he would adjust his recommended rate for the firm's contribution. If, for example, salary increases were racing ahead faster than expected, he would recommend an increased contribution rate. On the other hand, if the scheme's investments had been performing exceptionally well, he might be able to recommend a reduction in contributions.

In short, the actuary monitors what happens and makes recommendations for adjustments when he sees fit. He also assesses the extra outlay needed if the firm wants to improve benefits in some way. He is a professional independent of the firm he is advising and he usually works for a firm of consulting actuaries, a pensions consultancy firm or an insurance company.

If the employer wishes, the actuary can take the opportunity during the course of these regular assessments of the scheme, to see if there is any room to improve the benefits, most especially by uprating pensions already being paid. He first calculates what he regards as the value of the scheme's liabilities and assets. If the assets are larger, he might recommend that part of the resulting surplus is spent increasing payments in all current pensions, including widows' and widowers' pensions.

THE TAX RELIEF SYSTEM

The most obvious tax relief for you as an employee is that you pay your contributions to your firm's scheme out of your pay, *before* tax is assessed. In effect the contribution reduces your taxable pay, and thus the tax you actually pay. For example, the 5 per cent contribution on earnings of £200 costs you, on the face of it £10, because it reduces your taxable pay by £10, you end up paying £2.70 less tax. So the actual *net* cost of your £10 contribution is only £7.30. If you earn a lot more and would normally pay tax at higher rates, you save even more.

No less important are the other tax benefits. No income or capital gains tax is levied on the amount that your own and the firm's invested contributions earn. Also, your firm's contributions are treated as a business expense.

These three elements taken together make a tax-approved pension scheme far and away the most tax efficient way of saving for your retirement. Exactly the same is true with regard to money purchase schemes and personal pensions.

However, in exchange for these valuable reliefs, the scheme has to comply with rules set by the Inland Revenue. The rules include limits of the benefits that can be paid by the scheme. These rules are complex and their details change frequently, they can be summarised as follows:

PENSION RULES

● You must not have an occupational pension which amounts to more than two-thirds of your final pay. And it must be less than that if you cannot complete very many years with your firm before retiring.

TAX TREATMENT OF PENSION CONTRIBUTIONS

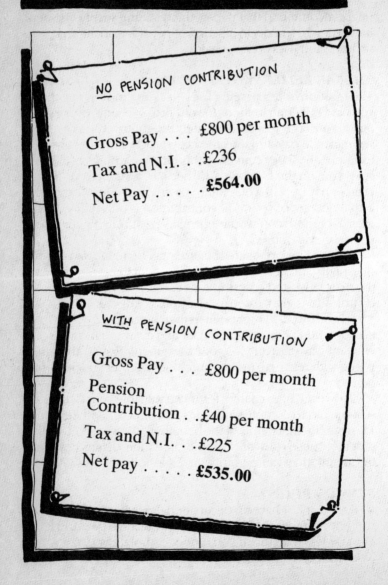

NO PENSION CONTRIBUTION

Gross Pay . . . £800 per month

Tax and N.I. . . .£236

Net Pay **£564.00**

WITH PENSION CONTRIBUTION

Gross Pay . . . £800 per month

Pension
Contribution . .£40 per month

Tax and N.I. . . .£225

Net pay **£535.00**

● You must not take a tax-free retirement cash sum of more than 18 months' pay – and less than that if you don't put in a full career with the firm. For anyone who entered a scheme after 17 March 1987 there's also a ceiling of £150,000, though for a good many years this will only affect people with exceptionally high earnings.

● Your wife or husband must not inherit more than two-thirds of your maximum permissible pension if you die first, although your dependants as a whole can inherit all of it.

● They cannot receive more than four years' pay, plus a return of your contributions, as the lump sum if you die before retirement age.

● You cannot withdraw your contributions at any time unless you leave your firm with less than two qualifying years completed, and you have to pay a 10 per cent tax bill.

● Your own contributions must not exceed 15 per cent of your earnings.

● Your firm is not restricted by a percentage ceiling. However, if the firm with a final salary scheme has been paying at so high a rate, or if investment conditions have been so favourable that the scheme's assets are more than 5 per cent larger than its liabilities, this surplus must be cut down quickly (or the scheme may lose its tax exemptions). This often means that the firm temporarily reduces or suspends its contributions. This is known as 'contribution holiday'. In recent years several large companies have been reported as being able to afford such 'holidays', although some of them spent part of the surplus on improving benefits for pensioners and current members.

In general, these rules and limits are not at all irksome for most employees. The main reason most people do not exceed the limits is that they and their firms could scarcely afford the money to do so.

A new kind of scheme – a 'simplified money purchase scheme' – doesn't have to adhere to some of the limits applied to what you can receive. For example, provided the total contribution paid by employee and employer is not more than 17.5 per cent of earnings, there is no limit on the pension.

ADDITIONAL VOLUNTARY CONTRIBUTIONS (AVCs)

Most occupational pension schemes have the facility for employees to boost their pensions (within Revenue limits) by making extra, fully tax-deductible contributions. The main rule governing contributions is that they should not take your total contribution over the 15 per cent earnings limit.

Employees may have a variety of reasons for paying AVCs: for example, they may be exceptionally keen on building up the best possible pension for themselves; the scheme to which they belong may offer a poor level of benefits; or, most importantly, they may have little to show by way of pension rights from previous jobs and have some catching up to do. Most AVC payers choose a set monthly contribution. But if the scheme's rules allow you can vary the payment, for example by investing a bonus payment straight into the AVC account.

AVCs usually work like this. You arrange with your firm to have the extra contribution you decide on deducted from your pay. It is then invested in an account of your own which will grow and be yours to spend on boosting your pension, arranging for cost-of-living increases on it or buying an extra pension for your wife or husband if you die first. AVCs paid into public sector schemes usually buy you 'added years', meaning that your pension is calculated on the basis of more years than you actually put in before retirement.

Here are two simple examples of the usual AVC method:

John Smith is 40 and a member of a pension scheme giving a pension of one-eightieth of final salary for each year worked. He joined the scheme when he was 35 and will retire at 65. He currently earns £10,000 a year and has no pension rights from a previous job. To qualify for full tax relief the maximum pension he is allowed by the tax authorities on his current earnings is £6,667 a year. His expected pension from his scheme is £3,750 a year (30/80 x £10 ,000). So the extra pension that could be provided by paying AVCs is £2,917 a year.

But how much would this cost him? He has 25 years to go before his retirement, and in fact he would only need to contribute an extra 5 per cent of his salary to fund the extra pension. This would mean an extra contribution of £42 per month, and an actual net cost after tax relief of only £31.

Eric Jones is 55 and a member of a good pension scheme giving a pension of one-sixtieth of final salary for each year worked. He joined the pension scheme 30 years ago and he will retire at 60. He currently earns £12,000 a year. The maximum pension he is allowed by the tax authorities on his current earnings is £8,000 a year. His expected pension from his pension scheme is £7,000 a year. (35/60 x £12,000). So the extra pension that could be provided by paying AVCs is £1,000 per year. He has only five years to go before he retires, so he would have to pay an extra 8 per cent of his salary (costing £80 a month gross, but only £58 net after tax relief) to finance the extra pension of £1,000 a year.

How AVCs are invested varies from scheme to scheme. They are mostly invested in some outside institution selected by the trustees. Their choice is often an insurance company offering a with-profits policy or unit-linked contract. It could

35

even be a building society's deposit account. Or it could be all three, so letting you make a considered choice, depending on the degree of risk or security you prefer while looking for a good investment return. Wherever the AVCs are invested, they get all the tax benefits enjoyed by the overall pension scheme.

You can also pay AVCs independently of the scheme you belong to. These are then called 'free-standing' AVCs. People usually want to do this because they think their scheme's choice of AVC investment is not wide enough, or because they believe they will get a better return from their investment by going to, for example, an insurance company they choose themselves. The tax authorities insist on a close liaison between the outside AVC provider and your firm's pension scheme to prevent you from paying too much or getting too much pension. But this should not affect you directly.

If you started paying AVCs for the first time after 7 April 1987, whatever kind of AVC you go for, the tax authorities will not let you use your AVC account to produce your tax- free cash at retirement. You will still be able take your cash, but it must come from your firm's occupational scheme.

WHAT 'CONTRACTING-OUT' MEANS

When any government sets up a new State pension scheme, it can decide that every working person has got to pay into it regardless, or that, if you belong to an occupational scheme providing pension benefits which reach a certain standard, then you can opt out of the State scheme and pay less National Insurance as a result. Opting out in this way is known as 'contracting-out'.

In 1978, when SERPS was introduced, the government took the latter course. It gave you the option of contracting-out if your existing pension arrangements were good enough. In effect, employers running occupational schemes were able to declare that they wanted their pension scheme members to be contracted out of SERPS. One of the legal requirements was that they had to consult their employees' trade unions, though employers had the final word on the subject. In fact, some employers went so far as to ask their pension scheme members to vote on the subject. At the last count, more than 10 million employees out of the 11 million or so covered by occupational schemes chose to contract-out. In exchange for not being full members of SERPS, they naturally paid less National Insurance contributions. So if you are contracted out through your firm's pension scheme, your National Insurance contributions each pay day are 2 per cent less on whatever you earn between £41 and £305 a week (1988-89 rates) than those who stayed in the SERPS scheme.

A second requirement was that your firm's scheme must guarantee that neither you (nor your widow or widower) could be worse off than if you had been a full SERPS contributor. If you have ever come across the term 'guaranteed minimum pension' this simply means the pension which SERPS would have provided if you hadn't been contracted-out. Nearly always, as it turns out, the occupational scheme gives you and your wife or husband a larger amount.

But it is not just a guaranteed minimum pension that your firm's occupational scheme has to provide. If you change jobs and leave your pension rights behind, it also has to protect these against inflation up to your retirement. Your occupational scheme also has to share in the job of protecting your pension against rising prices after you have started to draw it. For your employer, contracting-out meant a saving in National Insurance contributions too, so your firm is paying 3.8 per cent less each pay day.

On the whole, contracting-out makes good sense for everyone concerned. If you are in an occupational scheme which is not contracted-out it is probably because it is quite small or because the workforce generally is older than

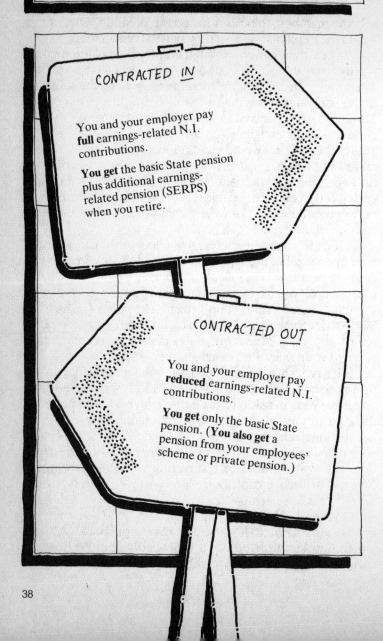

CONTRACTED IN

You and your employer pay **full** earnings-related N.I. contributions.

You get the basic State pension plus additional earnings-related pension (SERPS) when you retire.

CONTRACTED OUT

You and your employer pay **reduced** earnings-related N.I. contributions.

You get only the basic State pension. (**You also get** a pension from your employees' scheme or private pension.)

average or includes many women. Looking after these guaranteed minimum pensions would not have made good financial sense for private pension schemes.

From July 1988, the option to contract-out of SERPS has been extended to include occupational schemes which would not, or could not, have qualified before. In addition, from April 1988, individuals who do not belong to an occupational scheme, but who make their own pension arrangements, qualify for contracting-out. This is a radical change and will have far-reaching implications for the millions of people who are self employed or whose companies do not run any kind of occupational pension scheme. Chapter 5 and 6 explain how contracting-out will work from now on.

CLOSURE, MERGER AND TAKEOVER

Unfortunately a pension scheme sometimes has to close down. One of the main reasons for this is that the firm operating the scheme has gone out of business. In such cases, provided there have been no irregularities over the payment of employees' and employer's contributions into the pension fund, there may be a large sum of money which the trustees of the scheme must allocate between all the scheme members. Regrettably, this often takes a great deal of time, but eventually you should get a statement showing your share of the fund in the form of pension rights at retirement. How much this is depends primarily on the financial state of your firm's scheme when it closed down. It may have had enough assets to cover, or more than cover, the pension rights you had built up over the years. But,if there were insufficient assets, your pension rights would be disappointingly reduced although you would still get a fair share of what was available.

The other main reason for a closure is company merger or other reconstruction. For example, the company you work for may be taken over and its pension scheme amalgamated with that of the new parent company. This can sometimes work to your disadvantage. For example, you may be told that your scheme is to close down and that pension rights you have built up will be preserved rather than transferred to the parent company's scheme. In that case, you're being treated no better than if you had simply changed jobs.

Mostly, though, the post-merger deal is either advantageous or neutral in its effect on your pension rights. Here are some examples:

● The parent company has a policy of leaving its subsidiary companies alone over pensions and so decides to let your scheme carry on just as it is. One possible drawback with this is that there may not be quite the same commitment periodically to improve benefits in the future.
● The parent company invites you to join its scheme and, if you accept, will credit you with the same number of years' contributions as exist in your current scheme. If the parent company's scheme is better without costing you much more than you pay already, then this is an attractive offer – especially if you're guaranteed at least the pension you would have received from your current scheme.
● The parent company might take the best features of its own and your scheme and combine them in a brand new scheme for all its employees, so benefitting everybody.

There are several variations on these examples and the parent company should explain the pros and cons of its offer to you very carefully. Often, though, a merger or take-over is rushed through without too much thought being given to the pension scheme – and, to the employees, pension rights look less important than keeping one's job. Sometimes, however, the parent company will have given a great deal of thought to the subject, much of it being positively unwelcome. Occasionally, there's a kind of 'pension asset-stripping' meaning that the parent company plans to close your pension scheme down and arrange for the fund surplus (which is what mainly attracted them to your company) to be shifted into its own business, just as if it were valuable real estate.

· 4 ·

YOUR RIGHTS WHEN YOU CHANGE JOBS

If an employee leaves a job which carries a pension, he is called an 'early leaver'. Most people agree that early leavers have been poorly treated over their pension rights by comparison with people who stayed in the same job. When they left they were often given 'frozen pensions' which couldn't be drawn until retirement age. In the meantime the frozen pension lost much of its value to rising prices. If you have a frozen pension from a previous job, it will probably stay frozen unless your old firm decides to uprate it.

However, new legislation in the early 1980s has improved things. If you change your job again you will lose less. The main result of the new legislation is that while your ability to take your contributions back is severely limited, your pension rights earned so far are better protected. There is extra protection against inflation and new options over where your pension rights should be kept for you.

If you leave for another job after contributing to your firm's scheme for less than two years, you can probably withdraw only a proportion of the contributions you have paid in yourself. You can't take the whole amount.

For instance, if you paid the lower rate National Insurance contribution because you were contracted-out of the State earnings-related pension scheme, you would be brought back into SERPS as if you had never been contracted-out. That means you would have to repay (out of your returned contributions) the saving you made on your National Insurance contributions. Also, whatever you are entitled to take out is liable to a 10 per cent tax bill as compensation for the tax relief on your contributions.

THE CHOICES OPEN

But if you have been a member of your firm's scheme for two or more years you can't withdraw the contributions you have made since April 1975. You could take out any earlier contributions, but you might find something deducted for National Insurance and there would certainly be the 10 per cent tax bill. Instead you are given the right to a 'preserved pension'. There are three ways in which you can exercise this right:

Option 1 – A preserved pension

You can leave your preserved pension behind in your present scheme. For example, if you have been in the scheme for six years and your current pay is £9,000 a year, the preserved pension formula is probably going to be six-sixtieths of £9,000. This would give you a pension of £900 a year, kept for you until you reach the scheme's retirement age. By then, however, it will have grown to more than £900 per annum in cash terms – though the money may still buy less than it would today.

Part of this pension entitlement will go up in line with average earnings or by a fixed rate because it's the equivalent of what SERPS would be giving you if you hadn't been contracted-out.

Another part – roughly the amount you had built up since January 1985 – will by law go up in line with price rises, but with a maximum of 5 per cent a year. And, possibly, the rest of it will go up too because your scheme may be the generous kind which gives discretionary increases when the money is there to spend on early leavers like yourself.

It's a complex picture, but it is much better than the old system when a pension would stay frozen at the same level until you retire. You won't know exactly what you will be getting until you reach retirement, but provided inflation stays low you will be reasonably well protected. And you can

In future the job-changer's preserved pension from each previous employer will increase in value by up to 5% a year. This will make

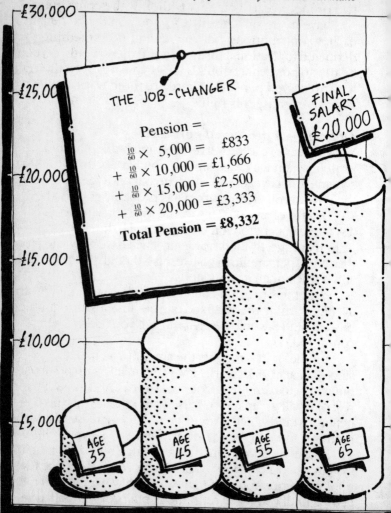

THE JOB-CHANGER

Pension =

$\frac{10}{60} \times$ 5,000 = £833

$+ \frac{10}{60} \times$ 10,000 = £1,666

$+ \frac{10}{60} \times$ 15,000 = £2,500

$+ \frac{10}{60} \times$ 20,000 = £3,333

Total Pension = £8,332

FINAL SALARY £20,000

AGE 35

AGE 45

AGE 55

AGE 65

the picture brighter – but still not so bright as for the one-company man.

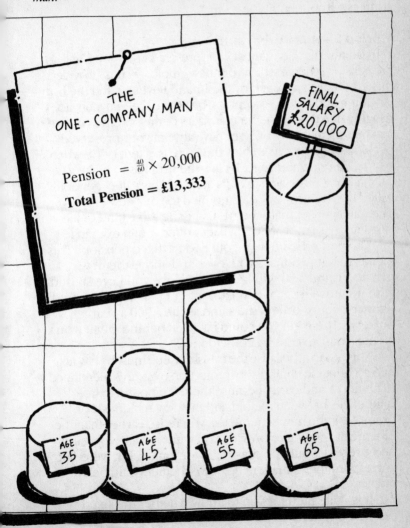

THE
ONE - COMPANY MAN

Pension $= \frac{40}{60} \times 20,000$

Total Pension = £13,333

FINAL
SALARY
£20,000

AGE
35

AGE
45

AGE
55

AGE
65

expect your old firm to get in touch with you shortly before you reach retirement age – unless you have changed your address without notifying them.

Option 2 – A transfer value

You can transfer the value of your preserved pension rights to the pension scheme which your new employer runs, provided this scheme is approved by the Inland Revenue and the firm is willing and able to accept it. The sequence of events goes roughly like this. First, the managers of the scheme you are leaving calculate the present-day value of your preserved pension of £900 a year (plus the increases to it), due when you reach retirement age. By law the firm has to make a fair calculation on the advice of its actuary. This value, generally called the 'transfer value', is notified to your new employer. The managers of that scheme, using the same kind of fair calculation, then work out what to offer you in exchange.

The new scheme might offer you a 'fixed pension'. This means that it promises you, over and above the new pension rights you will be earning once you have started with the new firm, an extra amount of pension. It should be worth more or less the same as the £900 a year preserved pension you could have left behind, but it won't be the same, except by coincidence.

This is partly because the transfer value must by law take into account the compulsory protection measures mentioned in Option 1 and partly because there are bound to be differences between the old and the new schemes. For example, if the new scheme lets you retire earlier than the old one, it is going to provide you with a smaller pension because you would be drawing it for longer. If it were not correspondingly smaller, the new scheme would be out of pocket.

It is quite hard for you to know whether this fixed pension offer is as good as the preserved pension which you could leave behind. But the law demands that it should be a fair offer and you should feel able to accept it with reasonable confidence.

Alternatively, the new scheme might offer what are often called 'added years'. This means that your transfer value is converted into a set number of extra years which will, in the calculation of your final pension, be added to the years you are going to work up to retirement with your new firm. But you shouldn't expect that the six years (going back to the example again) in the old scheme will earn you six years with the new scheme, unless you have negotiated a very special deal with the new firm. It may only offer you, say, two-and-a-quarter added years.

The reason for this is that your six years produce a pension for you which was worked out on your salary when you left your old firm. But your pay when you retire from your new firm is bound to be larger because of inflation, real pay rises and possibly promotion. So two-and-a-quarter added years is likely to be a fair exchange for your transfer value when it is used to produce a pension based on your pay at retirement.

Again, it is hard to judge how good the added years offer is, but it has to be reasonably and fairly calculated. In fact, if you ended up with a pay figure at retirement which was bigger than expected at the time of transfer, you would have profited on the deal. Many people who have accepted an added year's offer have profited in this way, simply because their salary at retirement has worked out substantially higher than was assumed when the offer was made.

Option 3 – A 'buy-out' plan

You can arrange for the same transfer value as in Option 2 to be paid into an individual insurance policy, often called a 'buy-out' plan. With this, the insurance company of your choice invests your transfer value (less the expenses it needs

47

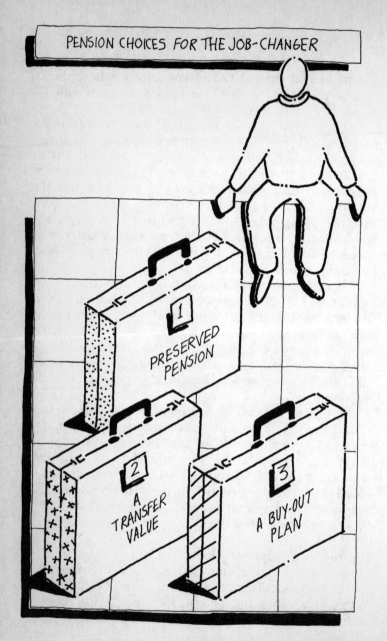

PENSION CHOICES *FOR* THE JOB-CHANGER

1 PRESERVED PENSION

2 A TRANSFER VALUE

3 A BUY-OUT PLAN

to set the policy up) so that the proceeds can be used to buy pension and other benefits for you at retirement. In the last few years, this approach has proved very popular because it can produce a bigger pension in terms of its eventual purchasing power than the preserved pension you would have left behind.

How much bigger depends on the insurance company's investment performance, on economic conditions generally, and on whether you choose a low-risk kind of investment (one with guarantees) or a higher-risk one (a unit-linked one, for example) where the return could be greater.

Taking up a 'buy-out' plan (or a transfer to your next firm's scheme as in Option 2), usually means that your old scheme loses all interest in you. You have gone 'off the books' and so will be left out of any programme to give a general discretionary uprating to the pension rights which early leavers left behind. Even so, that could be only a small risk compared with the gain made by taking up a 'buy-out' plan.

For example, an insurance company quotation using common assumptions about investment returns might predict (not the same as guarantee) that you would end up with a pension of £1,800 a year, rather than £1,500 a year into which the £900 a year preserved pension in Option 1 could be expected to grow.

From July 1988, a further alternative to a 'buy-out' plan, and one which works in practically the same way, is to have your transfer value moved into a personal pension plan. You might choose this alternative if you decided not to join your next firm's scheme or because it doesn't have one to offer you. A personal pension scheme is yours and yours alone – whoever you are working for – so it enables you to overcome the problem of transfer values next time you change jobs.

The big question is: given these three options, which one should you choose? The decision is entirely yours. In theory, they should all add up to the same end result, because the starting point for each of them is the same preserved pension rights you have earned in the scheme you are leaving. In practice, however, taking a transfer will often produce a noticeably better result for you – if you transfer to your new employer's scheme, this is likely to have your interests more at heart than your previous employer's scheme. If you use the 'buy-out' pension route your personal pension rights are at least under your control.

But it is, of course, in your own interest to compare the answers which each option produces. This needs some care because you may find you're not comparing like with like. For example, one pension on offer may carry an automatic widow's pension, post-retirement increases and even an earlier retirement age, while the other may not. Not too easy a comparison, but what's at stake is at least two years' worth of pension rights – and it could be much more than that. Sometimes you will be lucky enough to find that the pensions managers at the firm you are leaving or at the one you're joining will be happy to set out the figures for you. They may even organise some expert advice to guide you towards whichever option looks most promising. If not, you can always pay for advice in much the same way as you may have paid a solicitor or an accountant to advise you in the past.

This kind of personal advice might cost you around £200. You can obtain a list of pensions advisers from the Institute of Actuaries (Faculty of Actuaries in Scotland) or the Society of Pension Consultants. Their addresses are at the back of this book.

THE PUBLIC SECTOR
This chapter has largely focussed on people who work in the private sector. Special procedures apply to people who change jobs within the public sector. For them it is a lot simpler. A local government worker might go to work for

another local authority or become a civil servant, and because he is staying in the public sector, it is customary for his pension rights to go with him to his new job. This means, that at retirement his pension is calculated as if he worked for the same employer throughout. So public sector employees don't have the same kind of decisions to make when they change jobs unless they leave the public sector for a job in the private sector. In that case they too have the same three options described earlier.

DEATH BENEFITS
One important question often overlooked when someone changes jobs is what happens to the death benefits?

When you leave a scheme, your death benefits – which may be a lump sum of two years' pay or more, plus a life pension to your wife or husband – nearly always stop immediately. If you are going to be covered by the scheme your new firm runs (and only a short gap occurs before that cover starts) you do not have too much to worry about. But if the gap is going to last for a long time or if your new job doesn't carry a pension scheme with death benefits, it makes sense to take out some cover on your own account.

If the scheme you are leaving uses an insurance company to provide the death benefit cover, you may be allowed a month to decide whether to continue the cover at your own expense – on its usual rates but without the need to provide evidence that you are in good health. Otherwise, it's up to you to look around for an insurance company of your own.

· 5 ·
CHANGES IN THE
UK PENSIONS SYSTEM

In the early 1980s the government took a long, hard look at the way in which pensions are organised for the employed. A review carried out by the social services secretary led him to three main conclusions.

The first was that State pensions, particularly the State earnings-related pension (SERPS) which was then in its infancy, would prove to be a heavy and perhaps unendurable burden on working people in the next century. The reasoning was that SERPS would begin to deliver its fully matured pensions at a time when the ratio of National Insurance contributors to pensioners was falling from rather more to rather less than two-to-one. This population change is largely due to the baby boom which occurred in the few years after the end of the World War II. The government concluded that it was not viable to expect the children and grandchildren of today's working people to pay for bigger State pensions for them in 30 or 40 years' time.

The second conclusion was that people should be given the opportunity to build up pension rights of their own independently of the State system. If they preferred, they should also have the right to build up pension rights independently of their firms. Pensions, in other words, need not be thought of any differently from the right to buy council houses or the privatisation of State enterprises.

The third conclusion was that, after 30 years of growth, private pensions coverage through occupational schemes run by employers had levelled out to affect about half the working population. Any steps which could start private pensions coverage growing again would therefore be useful. So, in its 1986 Social Security Act, the government legislated for quite radical changes. This is a piece of complex law, but the main ways in which it affects you are these.

THE BASIC STATE PENSION

This is unchanged, with the full flat-rate, State pension paid to everyone with a sufficient National Insurance contribution record, plus an extra amount for married couples. (If you are in any doubt about whether your record is adequate, ask at your local Social Security office.) As before, it remains the only way for self-employed people to build up an entitlement to a State pension.

But, as explained in Chapter 1, the basic State pension is linked only to prices, not to average earnings. As earnings are tending to rise faster than prices, this means that although the pension will always be able to buy the same goods and services, the prosperity gap between retired and working people will steadily widen. If you are in your 20s or 30s now, in 30 years' time it will probably amount to about 10 per cent of an average worker's pay, instead of the 20 per cent it is at present – unless it is substantially raised by a future government.

THE STATE EARNINGS-RELATED PENSION SCHEME

The benefits available from SERPS pensions are to be cut back sharply. Eventually their value will be about half what they were originally intended to be. The cuts are three in number.

Firstly, the pensionable earnings which are used in the pension calculation are not to be the average of your best 20 years' earnings out of your whole working life since 1978. Instead, they are to be the average of all your years worked since 1978. In all cases this will give a lower figure and for some people a much lower figure. Secondly, your maximum pension will not be 25 per cent of your average pensionable earnings. Instead, it will be 20 per cent and may be even less if you have not always been employed since leaving school.

And thirdly, the SERPS pension paid to the widow or widower of a SERPS contributor will be 50 per cent, not 100 per cent, of the contributor's pension.

None of these cuts will affect anyone retiring or widowed this century. But in 10 gradual steps from the year 2000 onwards they will affect everyone else.

Taken together, the basic and SERPS pensions as originally planned had broadly meant that someone on average earnings could expect a pension of around 40 per cent of final earnings at retirement age. Now, the expectation for people presently in their 20s is more like 20 per cent of final earnings. Very clearly, this is insufficient to live on adequately without some extra pension resources. And, as the next section shows, the Government is anxious for you to make extra provision, either on your own account or with the assistance of your firm in some way.

A NEW CHOICE FOR SERPS CONTRIBUTORS

From July 1988, if you do not belong to a contracted-out occupational pension scheme run by your firm, you can contract-out of SERPS as an individual. This means that your firm does not have to be involved in the decision. If you do this, you must take out a personal pension with an authorised supplier, such as an insurance company, a building society, a bank or a unit trust company.

But because you have resigned from SERPS the Department of Health and Social Security (DHSS) will pay direct into your personal pension scheme part of the National Insurance contributions currently paid by you and your firm. On top of this 'rebate' there will be an extra incentive payment lasting until April 1993 and some tax relief on your 'share' of the rebate.

For example, take a man earning £10,000 a year (his 'pensionable earnings' from the DHSS's point of view are £7,972) who contracts-out in July 1988. He is entitled to backdate this to April 1987, so for the 1987-88 tax year the DHSS payment into his personal pension is made up like this, shown first as a percentage of pensionable earnings and second as actual cash.

	PERCENTAGE PAYMENT	**ACTUAL CASH PAYMENT**
Rebate	6.25%	£498
Tax Relief	0.79%	£64
Incentive	2.00%	£159
Total	**9.04%**	**£721**

The percentage payments change every so often. For the five tax years starting in April 1988 the total percentage payment will be 8.54 per cent. From 1993, when the 2 per cent extra is no longer payable, it will probably be about 5 per cent for five years and so on until it eventually levels out at below 4 per cent.

The question you have to answer is: will you be better or worse off with a SERPS pension than with a personal pension? The answer depends very largely on your age and your sex. The DHSS's percentage payment is worked out on your earnings regardless of your age and sex and therefore favours younger employees more than older ones and men more than women.

Staying with the above example, a 25 year-old man receiving the £721 DHSS payment only needs an estimated £238 to cover the SERPS pension he is giving up. The remaining £483 buys him extra pension and is his 'profit' on the deal. But a 55 year-old man needs £827 to cover the abandoned SERPS pension, and so would make a 'loss' on the deal. The table shows estimates illustrating this point for a number of ages for the 1987-88 tax year.

Profit or loss table

| | Age | Profit (+) or Loss (−) | |
		Men	Women
Earning	25	+ 240	+ 208
£6,000 a year	35	+ 196	+ 146
	45	+ 115	+ 23
	55	− 53	− 112
Earning	25	+ 483	+ 418
£10,000 a year	35	+ 393	+ 292
	45	+ 230	+ 47
	55	− 106	− 225
Earning	25	+ 806	+ 697
£15,340 a year	35	+ 656	+ 488
	45	+ 384	+ 79
	55	− 178	− 376

Working out whether someone makes a profit or a loss depends on many predictions about the future. But it is generally reckoned that men under 45 or so in 1988 and women under 40 or so would do well to contract out of SERPS and take a personal pension. Later on, it will be sensible to see if it is still advisable to stay contracted-out. If it is not, they should contract back into SERPS.

There is no legal obligation for either you or your firm to pay anything else into the personal pension you take out. But anyone keen on building up a decent pension will need to pay extra contributions. Having contracted-out, you may be in line for a better pension than SERPS could give you, but that's not necessarily anything like enough to live on comfortably. Chapter 6 has more information on what it takes to accumulate an acceptable personal pension.

Employees who contribute to SERPS and are in their firm's pension scheme cannot contract out of SERPS and claim these DHSS payments. Even though they are young enough to benefit from contracting-out, they cannot because they are not eligible for a personal pension. But they can contract-out if they take out the kind of 'free-standing' AVC plan mentioned in Chapter 3. However, they may not get such good tax relief as with a personal pension.

A NEW CHOICE FOR OCCUPATIONAL SCHEME MEMBERS

If you're in your firm's pension scheme, you probably had no choice. You had to join as a condition of the job and you may have resented being forced to pay a contribution each pay day. (As you approach retirement, however, you may stop feeling resentful!) You're probably contracted out of SERPS too, meaning you pay reduced National Insurance contributions and are therefore guaranteed a pension from the firm which is at least as good and probably much better than SERPS. In this case you won't have had much choice about contracting-out.

The present government's opinion about all this compulsion, however much in your own long-term interests it may be, is that in the interests of freedom of choice it should stop. So now if you are in your firm's pension scheme you can resign from it. And if you are invited by your firm to join its pension scheme you can turn the invitation down.

But you must, by law, still take part in some pension scheme to build up pension entitlements. So, if you refuse your firm's pension scheme you must pay full National Insurance contributions and build up a SERPS pension. Or you must take out a personal pension which is contracted-out of SERPS and so qualify for the payments from the DHSS, though not, in some cases, the 2 per cent incentive described in the previous section. (In either case you can also make additional voluntary personal pension contributions.)

If all you wanted to do was to pay the smallest amount possible, resigning from your firm's pension scheme helps you to do just that. If you are on average earnings and you contract back into SERPS, your reduced rate National Insurance contributions of £14.82 a week would rise to the full amount of £18.00 a week. But your pension scheme contributions would disappear. If this contribution was 5 per cent of earnings of £10,000 per annum, the net cost would have been working out at £7.30 a week after tax relief, an amount now saved. As a result your pay packet would be £4.12 a week larger. (Some firms' schemes do not charge you a contribution at all, so the question of saving anything wouldn't arise.) And although you would earn no further pension rights in your firm's scheme you would still be entitled to the pension rights you had earned so far.

FURTHER OPTIONS

If, however, you are thinking instead about the option which is likely to deliver you the best pension in the most efficient way, you have several important points to consider – important not just for you when you retire, but for your family if you die prematurely. The best way to tackle these points is by thinking about two particular questions:

Which gives me the biggest pension – SERPS, a personal pension or the firm's pension?

If you stay in the same job or if you are 35 or more, the chances are that the firm's pension will be more than the SERPS or personal pension alternatives. The reason is that your firm pays most of the cost of its employees' pensions and increasingly subsidises the cost of your particular pension as you grow older. However, this won't invariably be true. You might find your employer is willing to pay a substantial contribution into your personal pension. In this case, a personal pension to which both you and your employer contributed might be a better alternative. A lot depends on how long you anticipate actually staying with your employer.

When you are young, an occupational pension scheme contributes very little on your behalf. It may even pay nothing and your own contributions may actually subsidise the pension costs of your older colleagues. In this case, provided you believe you won't be staying with your firm very long (ie not long enough to be subsidised in turn yourself), resigning from your firm's scheme and taking a contracted-out personal pension could be the sensible thing to do. But you would need to pay into your personal pension whatever you save by resigning. However, do check first that your firm's scheme hasn't made some special arrangement aimed specifically at improving things for younger employees, especially those who change jobs.

This 'evening-up' arrangement could mean a special guarantee that your pension rights will be based on your own contributions plus half as much again from the firm if this produces a better result than the ordinary pension formula. Alternatively, the firm might propose that employees up to age 40 or 45 won't build up pension rights directly based on their earnings – instead these will be based on the investment proceeds of their own contributions plus further contributions from the firm. Such steps are calculated to give you a better deal than before and reduce the attractions of a personal pension.

What else would I be giving up if I resigned from my firm's scheme?

Some firms take a hard line with employees who resign from their schemes. They might even adopt an extreme position, ruling that if you resign, they won't maintain your death-in-service lump sum and widow's (or widower's) pension; you won't be allowed to rejoin the scheme at a later date; you can't expect any special pension treatment if you have to retire early, even if it's because of ill health; they won't allow you to take the value of the pension rights you've acquired into a personal pension; and under no circumstances will they ever pay a contribution of their own into your personal pension.

Those firms taking the hard line may be forced by circumstances to soften their attitude as time passes. Others already adopt a softer approach. But the hard line need not worry you if you are going to change your job before long.

If however, you propose to stay with your present firm, it would be sensible to discover what their scheme means to do if you decide to quit. If it intends to take a hard line, check (especially if you are married with children or have other dependants) to see how readily you could replace the benefits you would lose by leaving the scheme.

It is fairly safe to predict that as time goes by more and more younger employees will equip themselves with personal pensions. When these employees move to a new job their determination to keep their personal pensions going will be so obvious to the new firm that it may freely offer a contribution of its own to the personal pension. With the government's commitment to giving everyone freedom of choice, occupational pension schemes will inevitably adapt themselves to the new circumstances in which individuals are able to exercise that freedom.

· 6 ·

PERSONAL PENSIONS

The type of pension which you can take out yourself if you are self-employed, or if you work for a firm without a pension scheme, has been around for a good many years. The new-style personal pension available from 1 July 1988 is not greatly different and works in much the same way.

You have to decide first how much you want to pay. At this point it makes sense to acknowledge that if you are to have the kind of pension you want you will have to think periodically about increasing your payments. Next you have to decide on the financial institution in which you want to invest your contributions. Insurance companies, building societies, banks, friendly societies and unit trust companies – all these are now licensed to run schemes for your pension contributions. You also have to decide what kind of investment you want, choosing between simple, safe deposit accounts at one end of the investment spectrum and unit trusts and unit linked contracts at the other. With-profits insurance policies lie roughly in the middle.

You will also have to take other decisions – for example, how much cover you want for the benefit of your family if you die before retirement. Normally, the cost of an immediate lump sum and a pension to your wife or husband comes out of the tax-relieved contribution you're allowed to pay into a personal pension.

If you are an employee, your retirement age is usually chosen for you. If you are self-employed you can virtually choose your own. But in any case you have to state at the outset the age at which you want to take your pension. You can change your mind later on, but it must be somewhere between 50 and 75. (In practice, most people go for 65 if they're men or 60 if they're women because that's when State pensions are first payable.)

PERSONAL PENSION PLAN

Prepared for **R. Jones Esq.**
Retirement age 65

Age next birthday: 30

YOUR OUTLAY

Your estimated benefits below are based on a total monthly outlay of:	£30.00
After tax relief of 27% your net outlay is:	£21.90
Your total net outlay over the term of the plan is:	£9,329.40

YOUR RETIREMENT BENEFITS – WITH PROFITS

Assuming that contractual annual interest and bonuses paid are equivalent to an "investment return" of 13% per annum the total estimated value of the fund is: £189,565.00

This could buy you a **full pension** for your lifetime of   £26,419.00

OR ALTERNATIVELY
(under current legislation)
A tax-free cash sum of: £59,010.00

PLUS
A reduced pension for your lifetime of: £18,190.00

THE EFFECT OF DIFFERENT GROWTH ASSUMPTIONS

"Investment returns" could be greater or smaller than assumed above.
The effect of a different return is shown below:

"Investment return"	11% p.a. compound
Total estimated value of the fund at retirement age:	£117,968.00

WHAT KIND OF BENEFITS?

By the time you arrive at retirement age, your invested contributions will have grown into a substantial sum of money. You then have your final pension choice to make: what retirement benefits should you spend this fund on? You can have some of it as a tax free lump sum. The rest must then be spent on buying a pension (properly called an annuity).

This annuity can be arranged so that part of it continues to your wife or husband in case you die first. It can also be arranged so that it increases regularly, for example by 4 or 5 per cent each year in line with rises in the cost of living. (Special rules apply if you have contracted yourself out of the State earnings-related pension scheme. For example, the pension built up from the DHSS payments cannot be paid out before the age of 65 for men or 60 for women. And the amount has to increase by up to 3 per cent each year, with half of it continuing to your wife or husband if you die first.)

Here's an example. A man with a wife five years younger than he is reaches 65 with a personal pension fund of £100,000. He decides to take a lump sum of £25,000 and buys an annuity of £6,000 a year with the balance of the fund. The annuity is paid monthly in advance and increases at 3 per cent a year. If he dies first, half of it will be paid to his wife, also with 3 per cent increases per annum.

Building up his retirement fund was done with the help of the tax authorities. Firstly, his contributions were allowed full tax relief at his highest tax rate. In fact, he deducted basic rate tax before he paid his contributions to his personal pension supplier. So, for every £100 he wanted to pay in, he only paid £73. The supplier claimed the other £27 from the tax authorities. He got any higher rate relief through re-coding after completing his annual tax return.

Secondly, no income or capital gains tax was charged on the investment profit his contributions made. And thirdly, his retirement lump sum was paid to him tax-free.

(As at January 1988)

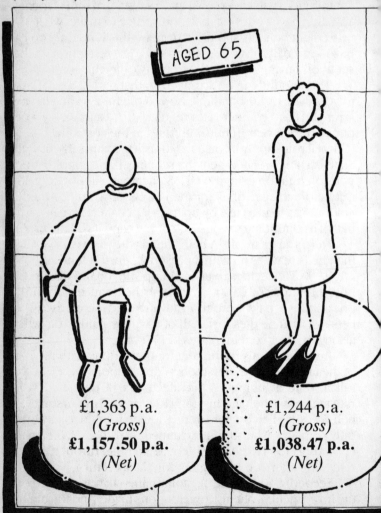

AGED 65

£1,363 p.a.
(Gross)
£1,157.50 p.a.
(Net)

£1,244 p.a.
(Gross)
£1,038.47 p.a.
(Net)

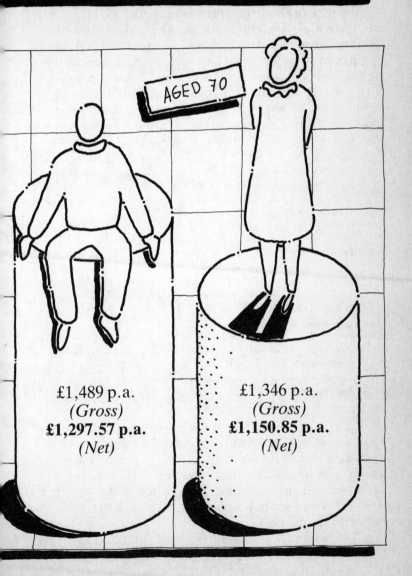

AGED 70

£1,489 p.a.
(Gross)
£1,297.57 p.a.
(Net)

£1,346 p.a.
(Gross)
£1,150.85 p.a.
(Net)

The important question here is: what does it cost to build up an adequate pension? The illustration below shows the fund which a man at various ages could expect to accumulate by paying £50 a month from now to age 65, along with the tax-free cash and pension he can expect. But it also shows what these figures amount to in terms of their purchasing power today. In other words, an adequate personal pension is one which buys an adequate supply of goods and services.

Age now	25	35	45	55
Contribution	£50 p.m.	£50 p.m.	£50 p.m.	£50 p.m.
Accumulated fund at 65	£180,300	£72,300	£26,500	£7,700
Tax-free cash	£45,075	£18,075	£6,625	£1,925
Annual pension	£16,800	£6,700	£2,400	£700
IN REAL TERMS				
Accumulated fund at 65	£26,240	£17,140	£10,230	£4,840
Tax-free cash	£6,560	£4,285	£2,557	£1,210
Annual pension	£2,430	£1,580	£940	£430

Figures like these have to be worked out on assumptions about the future. The two most important assumptions about the future are about investment growth (9 per cent per annum is assumed) and price increases (5 per cent per annum is assumed). Checking on these figures every so often will help you to see how important it is to increase your payments periodically.

The example above assumes a level contribution throughout, that is without increasing it in any way. The example that follows shows how much the ultimate rewards improve when contributions are increased by 5 per cent per annum.

Age now	25	35	45	55
Contribution	£50 p.m.	£50 p.m.	£50 p.m.	£50 p.m.
Accumulated fund at 65	£370,000	£119,000	£38,300	£9,300
Tax-free cash	£81,750	£29,750	£9,575	£2,325
Annual pension	£30,500	£11,100	£3,500	£800
IN REAL TERMS **Accumulated fund at 65**	£47,590	£28,210	£14,790	£5,850
Tax-free cash	£11,897	£7,052	£3,697	£1,462
Annual pension	£4,430	£2,620	£1,360	£530

Any personal pension owner has to stick to a number of Inland Revenue rules. In the following summary, the rules are those laid down by the 1987 Finance Act No 2.

● **Eligibility**   You can have a personal pension if you are between 16 and 75. But you cannot have one if you are currently a member of an occupational pension scheme run by your firm. If you have earnings from a second job, however, you may have a personal pension related to those earnings.

● **Maximum contributions**   There is no limit to the amount of pension you can draw from a personal pension plan, but there is a limit on how much you can pay in. This limit varies with your age, as follows:

Age at 6 April	Maximum percentage of reckonable earnings
50 or under	17.5 per cent
51 to 55	20 per cent
56 to 60	22.5 per cent
61 to 74	27.5 per cent

You can take up to 5 per cent out of these contributions to pay for lump sum death benefits, payable if you die before retirement. If you contract out of the State earnings-related pension scheme, the DHSS rebate payments do not count against these contribution limits but are in addition to them.

● **Employer's contributions**   So long as these maximum contribution limits aren't exceeded, your employer can pay into your personal pension too. It is safe to predict that over the next few years many more people will have their own personal pension than at present. It should follow that employers see their own contribution to new recruits' personal pensions as part-and-parcel of the remuneration packages they offer.

● **Maximum retirement cash**   On retirement you are allowed to take a tax-free cash sum of 25 per cent of the fund you have built up, though it can be less if you wish. This fund consists of both the voluntary contributions you've decided to pay and, if you have contracted out of the State earnings-related scheme, the DHSS's rebate payments. The 25 per cent would have to be reduced if it meant you were cashing in any of the rebate investment. The remaining 75 per cent must be used to buy yourself a pension. With this you may wish to include a widow's pension and index-linking, giving annual increases (see example on pages 70 and 71).

You can spend or invest the tax-free cash sum exactly as you please. Some people have a very clear idea of how they'll spend it, though most seem to deposit it where they can draw on it quickly until they see how their finances settle down.

There is just one other restriction. Your tax-free cash is limited to £150,000 from each personal pension scheme you belong to, although it is possible that the tax authorities will raise this figure every so often.

RETIREMENT AGE

Most working people have their retirement ages decided for them by their firms. The ages are usually 65 for men and 60 for women, but women have the legal right to work on as long as men doing the same job if they wish. These ages are usually chosen to fit in with the State pension age. But with a personal pension you can choose any age between 50 and 75. There is a qualification however. If you are contracted-out of the State earnings-related pension scheme, the benefits resulting from the invested DHSS rebates cannot be taken earlier than 65 for men and 60 for women. Although you have to choose a specific retirement age at the outset, you can always change it later on. In fact, few people want to take their benefits as early as 50. In any case, pensions intended to last a lifetime are expensive to buy if they start when you are so young. But you may find it an attractive option to take your tax-free cash and pension as early as this, since you can start contributions all over again at 50 – if you are still earning, assisted by the pension instalments – with a later retirement age in mind.

YOUR INVESTMENT CHOICE

How your pension contributions are invested is an important question. Obviously, how well the investments perform will have a profound effect on how well you're going to live in retirement. The first kind of choice is about investment type.

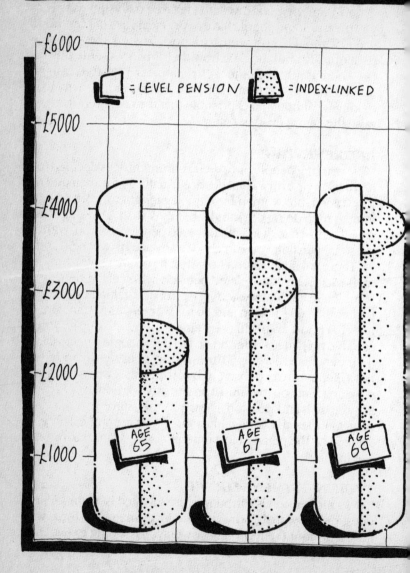

THE EFFECT OF AN INDEX-LINKED PENSION

= LEVEL PENSION   = INDEX-LINKED

£6000
£5000
£4000
£3000
£2000
£1000

AGE 65
AGE 67
AGE 69

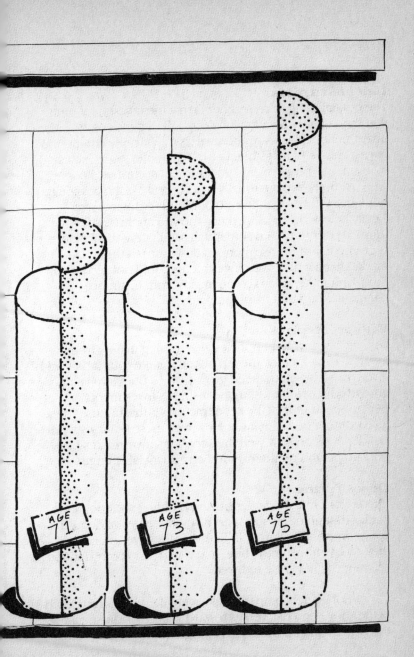

AGE
71

AGE
73

AGE
75

Unit linked plans

The crucial thing to remember is that the investment units you buy can go down as well as up. All depends on how the investment performs over the years to your retirement. You have a choice of investments – for example, stock exchange investments, property and government securities. People who favour these plans usually do so because of the possibility of higher returns than from other kinds of investment. Nevertheless, the risks are there and you might be advised to transfer your fund into something safer a few years before retirement, just in case there's a downturn in the stock market from which your investments could not recover in time. Unit linked plans come mostly from insurance companies and unit trust companies.

With-profits plans

Very like endowment policies and coming mainly from insurance companies, these plans guarantee your capital and give you both a guaranteed growth and a bonus-related growth which depends on the insurer's investment performance. One of the key attractions is that bonuses once given cannot be taken away. How well these bonuses work out depends on how well the supplier's investments have performed and on their underlying financial strength.

Deposit plans

These work much like deposits in building societies and banks, though other suppliers also offer types of deposit. Your contributions grow in line with the investment rates they declare from time to time, and your pension contribution account can never be reduced.

Although not comparing like with like, you can rate each of the above on a risk versus reward scale. Broadly speaking, the deposit plan is the safest, though in the long term it is

THE EFFECTS OF DELAYING THE START OF A PENSION PLAN

Both men contribute £40 p.m.

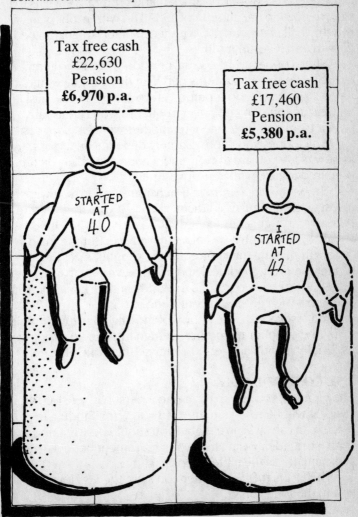

Tax free cash £22,630
Pension **£6,970 p.a.**

Tax free cash £17,460
Pension **£5,380 p.a.**

I STARTED AT 40

I STARTED AT 42

likely to perform least well. The unit linked plan is the least certain, but holds out the prospect of highest long-term growth, even considering stock market tumbles such as that experienced in the autumn of 1987. The with-profit plan is roughly half way between, with its elements of guaranteed growth and investment-links.

When you set up a personal pension you will be allowed to divide your contributions between different investments if you are unappy about putting all your eggs in one basket. So long as you don't do it too frequently, you can usually switch from one investment to another without extra cost.

Which ones you choose largely depends on factors such as how close you are to retirement and what risks you are prepared to take with your investments.

Choosing which personal pension supplier you want to invest with is a similarly difficult choice. If you organise your pension through an independent financial adviser he is legally bound to give you objective advice. But the main factors in making the choice are the supplier's general reputation for a good deal and good service; a proven investment track record; and the kind of underlying financial strength which gives you confidence.

You always have the option of moving your investment from one supplier to another, though this can be expensive, especially if you change soon after setting your plan up.

THE COST OF DELAY

The younger you start paying into a personal pension, the easier it will be to obtain the kind you want. Finding the money isn't always too easy, but you should bear in mind that even a brief delay can affect your retirement benefits substantially, as the table opposite shows.

The fact is that the sooner you start, the less it will cost you in the long run.

Cost of delay

Man planning to retire at 65 and investing £50 a month

His age next birthday	Loss in retirement benefits	
	After 1 year's delay	After 2 year's delay
25	11 per cent	21 per cent
35	12 per cent	23 per cent
45	12 per cent	23 per cent
55	15 per cent	29 per cent

· 7 ·

PENSIONS FOR THE SELF-EMPLOYED

Self-employed people are almost entirely on their own when it comes to building up pension rights. Their only entitlement is the basic State pension. This is £41.15 a week for a single person and £65.90 a week for a married couple – April 1988-89 figures – provided they have paid sufficient National Insurance contributions.

The self-employed get no State earnings-related pension (SERPS) unless they have worked for an employer for some period after April 1978 and contributed to SERPS. Nor do they get anything corresponding to a job-related occupational pension unless they have previously worked for a firm which ran a pension scheme to which they belonged and which is keeping some 'preserved' pension for when they retire.

If you are self-employed, you are dependent on your own resources for your pension just as you are for your business. Indeed, many believe that the business they run will itself become the source of their pension. They plan to sell it, stock, premises, goodwill and so forth, and live off the proceeds, maybe by buying an annuity or obtaining a regular income from investing the cash.

They may be right. But there can be problems with this way of planning for retirement. Plainly, a business which produces a high income while you're running it may not be worth so much without you at the helm. Indeed you may be the only real asset.

Alternatively, many self-employed people look ahead to a gradual withdrawal from the day-to-day running of the business with the idea of eventually acting in a consulting capacity. Again what may appear possible now can turn out to be both unworkable and tediously undesirable in the event. In this context, the self-reliance of the self-employed can be misplaced.

INVESTING IN A PENSION PLAN

The alternative is simple, even if sometimes financially painful. You invest some of your current earnings in a pension plan. In the absence of an employer and an occupational pension scheme, you have to create your own. However, there are compensations; in particular, quite significant tax benefits.

How much you need to invest (after making some allowance for selling your business) depends on your age and likely retirement age – the older you are the more you need to contribute. But you need to remember that each £1,000 per annum of a good pension – for example one which goes up by 5 per cent a year and of which half continues to your wife or husband if you die first – has to be bought with a lump sum. In fact, if you're a man and paid cash over the insurance company counter at 65, it would cost you about £13,500, and £16,000 if you're a woman doing the same at 60. Whichever way you look at it, this is a lot of money.

SECTION 226 RETIREMENT ANNUITIES

You may be already making contributions to a pension plan, usually called a 'Section 226 retirement annuity'. Like other kinds of pension plan, this qualifies for full tax relief at your highest rate of tax on the contributions you pay. Also, there is no income or capital gains tax to pay on the interest or capital gains made by your invested contributions. At retirement you can take part of the fund you have accumulated – around a quarter, sometimes more – as a tax-free cash sum. Alongside this pension plan, you may also be paying premiums – also tax-relieved – to the insurance company for life assurance cover.

When you take out a plan like this, you will probably have been told about the size of the fund you could expect to accumulate by your chosen retirement date, and what pension you could expect this to buy. These were and probably still are impressive figures. But you should have also been told that you could only assess their proper value by comparing them with your likely earnings at retirement.

There is a lesson in this. Because your earnings are probably going up each year, both in real and inflationary terms, you have to check every so often that you are paying enough contributions. Otherwise, your pension may be disappointingly small. And it's not quite enough to agree with yourself that you will pay the same percentage of your earnings (say 5 or 10 per cent). You will certainly find that as you get older you will need to increase the percentage to get the pension you want. You have plenty of scope to pay extra contributions without offending the tax rules – how much you are allowed to pay each year is shown in the table on page 68.

Moreover, there are two special incentives which particularly help self-employed people. First, a period of 12 months is allowed after the end of a tax year in which to pay a contribution to a pension plan and have it treated as if it had been paid in that year. Second, once the maximum permissible contribution for the current tax year has been made, you can bring forward 'unused' reliefs from the previous six years. In other words, the difference between the maximum reliefs for those years and the actual relief claimed is carried over. The tax reliefs then granted will relate to the personal tax rates for the current year.

PERSONAL PENSIONS

From July 1988, self-employed people can no longer take out Section 226 retirement annuities. Instead, they will take out the new 'personal pensions' which are described in Chapter 6. But if you're already paying into a Section 226 retirement annuity you can keep that going and, if it caters for increases, use it for the extra contributions you may decide to pay in the future.

Most self-employed people will probably decide to keep their existing plans going, partly for convenience and partly

CASH SUM AS % OF RETIREMENT FUND

MEN RETIRING AT...

60	65	70	75
29%	31%	34%	38%
25%	25%	25%	25%

SECTION 226

PERSONAL PENSION

WOMEN RETIRING AT...

60	65	70	75
26%	28%	31%	34%
25%	25%	25%	25%

SECTION 226

PERSONAL PENSION

because there's a particular advantage which the old Section 226 retirement annuities have over personal pensions. This concerns the tax-free cash sum at retirement age. Someone with a personal pension can take no more than 25 per cent of their accumulated fund in this way. But someone with a retirement annuity is restricted in a different way, because the tax rule says the tax-free cash must not be more than three times the remaining pension. Provided the annuity rates – these convert the value of your fund into an annual pension at retirement – are in your favour at the time, you could get more tax-free cash than 25 per cent of your retirement fund, as the table on page 79 shows.

However, the new personal pensions do have other advantages. For example you can draw its benefits as early as age 50 instead of 60 (the earliest age allowed for a retirement annuity). To many people, this is very appealing, even if they do not intend to stop work. It means that your contributions are not locked away for so long. Indeed, you could even take the benefit of the pension at 50, continue working, and start a new one! With all the tax advantages enjoyed by previous contributions, this beats practically any other form of savings!

If you have not taken out a pension plan by July 1988, then it is the personal pension outlined in Chapter 6 which you need to consider. All the rules there apply to you in the same way as to employed people whose employers make no pension provision for them. An exception is how you get your tax relief: you cannot deduct relief from each contribution you pay. Instead, you have to obtain it at the end of the tax year.

EMPLOYING OTHERS

However, there are some aspects of pensions which apply to self-employed people and no one else. Firstly, if you are married it's quite possible that your wife or husband is your employee. If your wife, for instance, is putting in anything like a full working week and is paid the proper rate for the job, then it's going to make good sense for her earnings to be pensioned as well as yours. This can be organised by you, as her employer, by setting up a simple pension plan into which you both, or just you, pay tax-relieved contributions. Your wife can organise it by taking out a personal pension in her own name into which she pays tax-relieved contributions. Chapter 6 explains how this works and Chapter 5 describes how, as a contributor to SERPS she could, if she is young enough, take advantage of the government's offer of special rebates of National Insurance contributions. These get invested in the personal pension she takes out instead of belonging to the State pension scheme.

As well as employing your wife or husband, you may employ other staff too on a more or less permanent basis. You can take it that the interest in pensions which recent legislation is generating may easily prompt them to ask you about organising pension rights for them. What that really boils down to is whether or not you are willing to pay a pension contribution on their behalf. If you are, then you have the option of either setting up a simple plan into which you and they contribute or of contributing to the personal pensions they take out by themselves. Again, your contributions and theirs would be fully tax-relieved.

BUSINESS LOANS

The second aspect of a pension plan which is particularly useful for self-employed people is the possibility of arranging a business loan on the back of it. For any businessman, obtaining finance can be a problem. But pension plans can provide a convenient and highly tax-efficient way of solving it, while simultaneously making the idea of 'locking' contributions away in a pension plan much more acceptable. This is because recently a new feature – generally known as a 'loanback' – has been introduced alongside personal pension plans.

So, what can 'loanback' actually do? The answer is that the 'loanback' facility can be extremely valuable in aiding the finance of your business. There are two distinct aspects to the loans available with pension plans.

Firstly, there is a loan facility by which a bank is prepared to lend money to a pension plan holder on terms which are often better than normal. This is because the bank is aware that the pension plan should provide sufficient tax-free cash at retirement to repay the loan. The advantages to your business are: the loan may be offered at a lower rate than otherwise; it may be offered over a longer term; and there is no need for the capital to be repaid until the pension plan matures. The amount available is based on a maximum multiple of 25 times the premium paid, reducing with age. Thus, investing in a pension plan can have the effect of actually increasing the cash you have available.

The second aspect is the actual 'loanback'. Although insurance companies operating pension schemes do not literally lend back money paid into personal pension plans, what is often available is the right to apply for a loan direct from the insurance company up to the full current value of the plan. A loan like this can be useful for a business because its availability is not affected by the credit restrictions sometimes placed on banks. Again, the investment in the pension plan has opened up a new source of loan finance for your business. However, the minimum loan is £5,000, so the pension plan either needs to have substantial contributions paid in, or else to have been running for some length of time in order to build up the necessary value. The loan itself will naturally need repaying, and if the plan holder wants to do this with the tax-free cash at retirement, then he also needs to ensure that there will be sufficient money in the fund to do so. The insurance company will also require security for the loan, usually in the form of a charge over private property.

With these different loan facilities, the two aims of personal and business finance can simultaneously be reconciled, at least in part. Your enthusiasm should be moderated by remembering that the prime purpose of the pension plan is to build up a big enough 'fund' to buy you a good pension. This pension should be big enough to enable you to retire in comfort. A loan that has to be repaid out of your pension fund at retirement is inevitably going to diminish your pension. So be cautious. If you borrow some money in this way, you should consider that the 'loan' must be invested in such a way that it will repay itself – in other words, it has to be a viable business proposition to warrant the risk of diminishing your retirement pension.

Personal loans, especially mortgage loans for house purchase, are another important aspect of pension plans. This is covered in Chapter 9.

· 8 ·

PENSIONS FOR WOMEN

In a perfect world with equality between the sexes, it wouldn't be necessary to have a separate chapter on pensions for women. But at present there are important differences in pensions treatment for men and women.

Both sexes clearly have in common a need for adequate retirement income. A man, traditionally but by no means exclusively the main bread winner, needs a decent income replacement when he stops work, especially if his wife is dependent on him. A single woman has the same need, especially if she has dependants. Similarly, a married woman who goes out to work needs an income to replace her earnings, however good her husband's pension is going to be, since the pair of them are usually accustomed to living up to the joint income they're getting while at work. Unhappily, she could find that if death or divorce removed him she would be left with all too little time to build up an adequate pension for herself.

It is therefore important that a woman, whatever her age and whether married or single, should never pass up the opportunity to pay pension contributions, whether they go to the firm's pension scheme or to a personal pension. This is also the case for some older married women and widows who have been paying reduced-rate 'married women's' National Insurance contributions which disqualify them from State pensions and several other Social Security benefits.

DIFFERENCES IN TREATMENT

The first important difference between men's and women's pension treatment concerns expectation of life. It is a statistical fact at present that the average woman lives longer than the average man. For example, on average the man who retires at 65 can expect to live for an average of another 13 years, while a women who retires at 60 can expect to live for another 20 years. The gap in life expectancy is evidently narrowing, partly as a result of more women undergoing stresses associated with taking paid jobs and then dying younger, but it still remains wide.

One implication of this is that women cost their employers more than men when it comes to providing a pension. That is something which most employers' pension schemes take in their stride. But another implication is that a woman who relies on a pension plan of her own needs to invest more to end up with the same amount of pension as a man. Conversely, it is cheaper for a woman to buy life assurance for herself or for her employer to buy it for her.

The second difference is pensionable age. The State pension system sets this at 65 for men and 60 for women. This is the earliest date at which a State pension can be drawn. There's little doubt that these ages will be equalised some time in the future, but lowering them will be expensive. One idea is that men and women should be free to draw State pension any time they like between the ages of 60 and 70. The effect of this idea would be that someone drawing a pension before the notional 'common pension age' of, for example 63, would get a reduced pension. Someone drawing it after 63 would earn a special bonus or increased pension. It is thought that many men would jump at the chance of taking a full pension at 63. But the expected cost of even this limited change would, in the government's view, be too expensive. In effect it would mean higher National Insurance contributions.

The sex discrimination law gives women the right to work on to the same age as men doing the same kind of job. In other words, the fact that her retirement age is 60 does not mean she can be compulsorily retired at that age. But she still has a decision to take regarding her occupational pension rights.

If her firm's scheme sets the pension age for women at 60 and for men at 65, she can either take her pension and tax-free cash sum at 60, or take the cash while leaving the pension until she actually stops work (it will have increased by then, the scheme rules say) or she could leave both the cash and the pension in the scheme until her retirement. Most occupational schemes will leave that decision to the woman concerned. But some insist that because she is still working she should continue to pay contributions, so earning extra pension in the same way as men. In that case, she wouldn't draw any benefits until she had finally stopped work.

STATE PENSIONS

Women build up their rights to the same basic flat-rate pension in nearly the same way as men. There are two important differences, one favourable to women, one unfavourable.

The favourable difference is that a woman who has to take time off work to look after young children or an elderly or incapacitated relative can claim Home Responsibilities Protection. This means that she is credited with the basic pension rights she would have accrued if still at work. A man can qualify for this protection too, but in practice it is usually the woman who has to give up her job for a caring role. The unfavourable difference is that although a man and a woman on the same earnings pay the same percentage National Insurance contribution, if she dies first her husband receives less help by way of a pension from her contributions than a man's wife will gain from his contributions if he dies first. This discrimination (which seems to hit both men and women simultaneously!) will probably be outlawed before too long because of EEC pressures to remove such anomalies.

The State earnings-related pension (SERPS) is built up in the same way regardless of sex, but again with the 'survivor pension' anomaly.

OCCUPATIONAL PENSIONS

The retirement age or pension age differential seen in the State system is usually carried over into occupational pension schemes too. Practically all women members of such schemes have 60 as their retirement age.

There is very little legislation which demands equality in occupational pension schemes between the sexes. However, women certainly have the right to join their employer's scheme on the same admission terms, such as the entry age and length of qualifying service, as men doing the same job. And a woman must be contracted-out of the State earnings-related pension scheme if her male colleagues are. But apart from that, inequality could legally run quite freely.

Happily, it does not do so to any very serious extent. In most schemes, you will find that men and women accumulate their pension at the same annual build-up rate, contribute the same percentage and, if they die before retirement, bequeath a lump sum to their dependants which is calculated in the same way. However, a few schemes still pay more out to a married man's dependants than to a woman's.

There are, nevertheless, two important differences in treatment. The first follows the lead set by the State pension system. Widowers are generally treated worse than widows. So, if you die before your husband, there may be no pension for him, though a widow would be able to draw half his pension whether he dies before or after retirement age. Or there may be a pension for your widower, provided he can show that he was financially dependent on you in the time before you died. Things are improving gradually, simply because it does not cost a scheme very much to treat widows and widowers the same.

The second difference is the amount of pension left over after you take your tax-free cash at retirement. The amount of cash would be the same for a man and a woman who have been earning the same for the same number of years in the job. For example the cash entitlement might be £9,900. But the woman retiring at 60 would usually have to give up only £900 a year of her pension to get the cash, while the man retiring at 65 would have to give up £1,000. This may seem odd but it's because the woman's earlier retirement age and greater expectation of life put a higher cash value on every £ of her pension.

Many occupational pension schemes exclude part-time workers, who are defined as putting in less than a certain number of hours each week. Often the number of hours is only marginally less than the hours calculated to make a full working week. This has the effect of excluding from the pension scheme much larger numbers of women than men. Along with differences in 'survivor pension' treatment, this is another topic regularly pursued by the Equal Opportunities Commission. Before long, it is very likely that pressure from the EEC or the EOC will bring in new legislation to equalise every benefit and option which occupational schemes contain.

PERSONAL PENSIONS

A woman has precisely the same opportunity as a man to contribute to a personal pension and obtain full tax relief. But because she would often choose an earlier retirement age than a man, usually coinciding with the earlier State pension age of 60 and because of her greater expectation of life, she must invest more than a man for the same pension. Take the example of a woman who proposed to retire at 60 on a pension of £5,000 a year and a man who wanted the same at 65.

To buy that level of pension, the woman would have to build up a fund of £48,250 in her personal pension account. By comparison, the man would need only £40,250. If, however, both wanted to provide half their pension for their husband or wife in case they died first, her account would need to be £49,700 and his £45,000. This supposes that in both cases the wives are years younger than their husbands. Again, it is the different life expectancies which lie behind the anomaly.

There is one exception to the statistically-based 'sexist' approach used by insurance companies when converting a pension account into an actual pension. When someone who has contracted-out of the State earnings-related scheme with a personal pension comes to retire, part of their pension account is 'derived' from the payments made by the DHSS into the personal pension. This part must by law be turned into pension on the same 'unisex' conversion rate. So the insurance company must on this occasion work out rates for men and women without any regard to their different life expectancies.

WIDOW'S PENSIONS

However straightforward the widow's pension seems to be, it is always worth checking the small print in the rules of an employer's occupational scheme. There may be special advantages or disadvantages inherent in the scheme.

The widow's pension paid if her husband dies before retirement is normally a proportion of the pension her husband would have received if he had survived through to his retirement age on his current earnings. Sometimes, and often more helpfully, it is a percentage of what he was earning when he died, such as 40 per cent.

Looking at the small print, however, you might find that there is an extra pension allowance for you while your children are young – up to age 16, 18, 21, or when they have finished their full time education. Although this is very helpful, it can sometimes mean that their education grant is correspondingly reduced. You might find that if you also die while they are young, the widow's pension you were drawing will continue to be paid to them in much the same way.

But you might also discover (and almost certainly would if your husband worked in the public sector) that your widow's pension would be suspended, reduced or stopped altogether if you remarried or even if you lived with another man as his common-law wife.

Also, you may come across a rule which states that if you are considerably younger than your husband (more than 10 years for example) your widow's pension will be reduced. Typically, this might be a 2 per cent reduction if you are 11 years younger, 4 per cent for 12 years, and so on. It is hard to see any justification for these rules and in the private sector they are gradually disappearing.

You would also do well to check when your widow's pension starts: is it immediately, or do you have to wait until five years after his retirement date? In the latter case it would be because you get an immediate payment of all the instalments of his pension remaining up to the end of the five years. Almost all occupational schemes pay out a lump sum when an employee dies before retirement age. Sometimes it is as much as four years' pay.

These small-print features may be included in the rules about the widow's pension which would be paid if your husband has retired and then dies before you do. The pension is likely to be a half of the one he was drawing or, more usually, half of the pension he would have been drawing if he had not exchanged part of his pension for a tax-free cash sum at retirement.

To avoid any liability for inheritance tax and to make payment as soon as possible the occupational scheme trustees have the final word over exactly how it should be paid.

The trustees have probably asked your husband to write down on an 'expression of wish' form where he would like the money to go, though they are not bound by what he has written. So it's up to him to keep the form up-to-date. You would do well to remind him of that. For example, if you

90

haven't been married long, there's a chance he may have overlooked changing the form from his mother's name to yours. If for some reason your name is not on the 'expression of wish' form, you should be able to rely on the trustees' good sense (and legal obligation to discover what dependants he has) to pay the money to you, the most deserving of your husband's dependants. Unfortunately, however, you do not have any legal right to know or alter what he has written.

These are rules which would be set by the scheme your husband belongs to at work. If he has a personal pension which he pays into by himself it's up to him to organise widow's benefits for you. You should therefore expect that part of the contribution he pays goes towards buying protection. This would take the form of a lump sum or pension (or both) for you if he dies before retirement age. In addition, the pension should continue at for example, half rate to you if he dies after retirement but before you. Unfortunately, not every husband provides for his wife in these ways. You cannot be completely sure unless you ask him to show you the details of his scheme.

YOUR RIGHTS ON DIVORCE

If your husband is obliged by a court order to pay you maintenance, the order would usually continue, though maybe for a reduced amount, after he has retired. But the difficulty comes if he dies before you do.

The State pays its widow's pensions only to legal wives and occupational pension schemes usually follow suit. So, what may be your main source of income would immediately dry up on your ex-husband's death. In time, the law may be changed to give an ex-wife some proportion of the widow's pension she forfeits at the time of the divorce. For example, it may be that if you were married to your ex-husband for half the time he was working for a particular firm you could claim half the widow's pension you would have qualified for if there had not been a divorce.

Meanwhile you do have some remedy. With your solicitor's help, you should be able to discover the present-day cash value of the widow's pension you are forfeiting. You can then apply to the divorce court at the time of the financial settlement for compensation for the pension loss. This compensation will come out of your husband's financial resources. If the court agrees with the cash value which you have calculated, it will then decide whether it should award it to you. If it does, the compensation may take the form of an immediate lump sum. Ideally, you should then invest it for your own retirement. But if you are proposing to get a job, or carry on with the job you are already doing, you would do well to make sure you are building up pension rights of your own in one of the ways described earlier in this book – through your firm's pension scheme or through a personal pension you take out yourself.

· 9 ·

PUTTING YOUR PENSION TO FURTHER USE

With rare exceptions, there is no way in which you can lay your hands on any of the pension contributions you have invested, or jointly invested with your employer, before you retire. You have to accept this restriction as your part of the bargain made with the tax authorities in exchange for the tax reliefs they give you.

PENSION MORTGAGES

However, it is possible, and these days it is increasingly popular, for people with a personal or employer-sponsored pension to use their pension as the basis for a loan, particularly a mortgage loan. This is so even though by law you cannot use your pension rights as collateral or security for a loan.

For a pension mortgage to be possible you have to belong to a pension scheme which pays out a tax-free cash sum as well as a pension when you retire. Nearly every scheme does just this. If you pay into a personal pension, the cash sum is around 25 per cent of the total fund you accumulate by retirement. If you are in your firm's pension scheme, the cash sum could be as much as 18 months' pay if you have put in 40 years service to retirement, about a year's pay if you put in 30 years, and nine months' pay, if you put in 20 years. Your pensions officer at work can tell you what your cash formula is.

Because you are in line for this cash sum, you should be able to find a lender, usually a building society or a bank, who is prepared to lend you up to about 80 per cent of its anticipated value. For example, if you can show that your personal pension's accumulated fund is going to stand at £200,00, you may be able to borrow around £40,000 to help buy your first house or move to a better one. You would pay

Assumes man age 40, standard tax rates and normal projections for pension funds and endowment policies.

Loan of **£30,000**

Net monthly outgoings **£307.00** (including interest and pension premium)

Loan repaid in 25 years? **YES**

Plus – Pension of **£24,000 p.a.**

And – Lump sum of **£47,000**

AN ENDOWMENT MORTGAGE

Loan of **£30,000**

Net monthly outgoings **£213**
(including interest and
endowment premium)

Loan repaid in 25 years? **YES**

Plus – Lump sum of **£14,000**

the lender interest on the loan all the way through to retirement and then pay the loan off in one go out of your cash sum.

This is broadly similar to the way in which endowment mortgages work. With them, you pay premiums to the insurance company and interest to the lender, leaving it until your endowment policy matures before you pay the loan off.

The important difference is that the pension contributions you pay attract tax relief with tax-free investment growth too, while the endowment premiums are either tax-relieved at a much lower rate or, if you took out the policy after April 1984, enjoy no tax relief at all. The real advantage of a pension-linked mortgage over an endowment mortgage (and a repayment mortgage too), is shown in the following example:

> Three men aged 40 – self-employed – each borrow £30,000 over a 25-year period.
>
> Mr A has a repayment mortgage which, after tax relief, costs him £235 a month. When he reaches 65, his loan will be fully paid off, but unless he invests in a pension plan he will only have the basic State pension to look forward to.
>
> Mr B has a 'low-start build-up' endowment mortgage, for which he pays £188 interest a month after tax relief, plus an initial endowment policy premium of £25 a month which attracts no tax relief. At 65, the loan will be fully paid off and he will also receive a £14,000 cash sum which he can spend as he pleases. But again, he will only have the basic State pension to live on unless he invests in a pension plan.
>
> Mr C has a pension mortgage and pays the same £188 interest each month, plus a pension plan contribution of £159 a month which nets down to £119 a month after tax relief. At 65 his loan will be fully paid off, but his pension contribution will produce a pension of £24,000 a year, plus a cash sum of £47,000 to spend as he pleases.

He is paying in total half as much again as the other two, but will end up with a very useful pension and cash sum, thanks largely to the tax relief given to his pension contributions.

Until a few years ago, the only people to take advantage of pension mortgages in any number were the self-employed. The fact that they had deliberately taken out a pension plan was in itself impressive in the eyes of lenders. Also, the insurance company which had arranged the pension plan often helped locate a lender who was prepared to allow an interest-only loan.

However, employees in their firms' pension schemes were not looked at quite so confidently – they had no option about belonging to the firm's scheme and, if they soon moved to a firm which did not run a pension scheme, there was no guarantee that they would take out a pension plan of their own.

Today it is different. Several firms of pensions consultants have entered the pensions mortgage market, offering to arrange lending facilities for employees belonging to their firm's pension schemes. Loans will naturally always be 'subject to status', meaning broadly that the lender has to be satisfied that you can manage the interest and pay off the loan when you retire. So you would have to answer the same kind of questions about your income as you would with an ordinary repayment or endowment mortgage.

Someone who takes out a pension-linked mortgage and later on changes jobs could have a problem if the lender doubts his ability to pay the mortgage off at retirement. It may then be necessary to switch the mortgage to a repayment or endowment type if the prospective retirement cash sum does not seem adequate.

It is usually a mistake to suppose that you can rely on what you are paying into your pension scheme to finance both a pension and a house simultaneously. Ideally, you need the pension to live on and the cash sum to draw on if necessary during your retired years. Passing the whole sum, or a large part of it, to the lender could leave you financially vulnerable. So, it generally makes good sense to increase your pension contributions if you have a personal pension or pay additional voluntary contributions if you are in your firm's pension scheme.

Home mortgages are the best example of loans taken out on the strength of a pension. Business loans, particularly for self-employed people, have been mentioned in Chapter 7. But lenders are prepared to advance loans for other approved purposes too, for example, fitting a new kitchen or buying a second home. Nevertheless, be cautious about committing any substantial part of your future pension to satisfy current whims.

· 10 ·
YOUR RIGHT TO INFORMATION

New pensions laws introduced in the mid-1980s have meant that people contributing to almost every kind of pension plan have the right of access to information about their plans. Armed with knowledge about your plan, you are in a better position to take action if it does not seem to be working as you expected. These information rules apply to both employer-sponsored occupational schemes, especially if they promise 'final salary' pensions, and personal pensions.

OCCUPATIONAL SCHEMES

Instances where an employer's pension scheme has failed to deliver its promised benefits are extremely rare. But in theory a scheme could fall on such hard investment times that its assets are insufficient to meet its liabilities. There is, in fact, a great deal of misunderstanding over the issue of adequate funding.

During the 1980s a combination of comparatively low pay increases (which largely determine the pace of increase in a scheme's liabilities) and comparatively high investment returns (which largely determine the pace of increase in a scheme's assets) led to most schemes being overfunded. This meant that if a scheme was discontinued, the pension rights built up so far for its members would be fully covered by the investment assets – and with a surplus.

But there have been times when the assets would not have covered those pension rights, with a deficit emerging instead of a surplus. The reason was sometimes that high rates of pay increases were accompanied by low rates of investment return. (This happened in the mid-1970s when inflation was rampant.) Nevertheless apparent deficits are not necessarily sinister. They may occur if your scheme is upgraded. Instead of earning, say, one-eightieth of your final pay for each year worked without any promise of guaranteed increases after you have retired, the scheme might decide you are, in future, to earn one-sixtieth for each year, including all the years you have worked so far, with your pension guaranteed to increase at 5 per cent a year.

The effect of this is to increase the scheme's liabilities very steeply. Your firm would probably be increasing its contributions, but it might be several years before the sudden deficit which the improvement created could be turned into surplus again. (The deficit could be removed at a stroke if the firm put in a large lump sum, but even highly profitable firms are rarely prepared to take the risk of jeopardising their commercial well-being by doing so.) In short, an apparent deficit need not be worrying, provided you know why it has arisen and what steps are being taken to remove it over a period of years.

To help you find out about your pension scheme, you have the right to see two important documents. Both of these are produced by the actuary to your firm's scheme. The first is a simple actuarial statement showing his yearly estimate of the scheme's assets compared with its liabilities. The second document, which is usually far more complex and unlikely to be easily mastered by the layman without help, is the valuation report. Usually this is produced every three years (or more frequently if there has been some significant change in the scheme's circumstances). Your scheme can make a charge for a copy of this document but it must be a reasonable charge.

If you and your colleagues – or your trade union, if it is recognised for collective bargaining purposes – find cause for concern in what you see in these documents, then it's up to you to pursue the matter with your firm. The government saw this as a better way of monitoring a scheme's finances than by imposing more or less rigid funding standards which could, in some cases, have persuaded firms that it would be sensible to abandon their schemes altogether.

The funding position is the most important piece of information about the scheme's finances and constitution. But you are entitled to more, for example:

● **A copy of the trustees' annual report**   This contains information about the scheme's investments and audited accounts as well as the general progress of the scheme over the past year. The trustees won't automatically supply you with this report, though in many cases they do so quite routinely.

● **A copy of the trust deed and rules**   These documents, often written in an impenetrable style by lawyers to satisfy the tax authorities, form the legal basis of the scheme and the benefits it promises. They show what the trustees' obligations are to the scheme members and all the circumstances in which benefits should be paid and options exercised. If you are going to take a close interest in the scheme, you must get hold of copies, for which you can be charged, though not an unreasonable amount.

● **A copy of the the scheme booklet**   This sets out in relatively simple terms the main rules about benefits and options. However, it won't necessarily tell you everything. For example, while it will describe the way in which your scheme promises to increase your pension after you have started to draw it, it usually won't say much about the discretionary increases it has been recently paying to retired people. You have to ask for that information separately – it should be in the trustees' annual report. Nor will it tell you in detail how much pension you will have to give up to get your tax-free cash at retirement. Again, you have to ask.

Others beside you can get hold of these documents too: recognised trade unions, employees who haven't yet joined the scheme, your wife or husband or anyone else who stands to benefit from the scheme. This is all general information and other more personal information is available to you as well:

● **A benefit statement** Although under no legal obligation to give you one unless specifically requested, a great many schemes automatically give you a prediction each year, as part of their computerised administration. The statement will summarise what your pension will be assuming that your present earnings stay unchanged. It will generally go on to say what your family would collect if you die, whether before or after retirement age. Alternatively, the statement might just confine itself to saying how much pension you have built up so far, or even just tell you how to work your pension out by yourself. But many schemes regard a comprehensive benefit statement as a useful reminder of the importance of your stake in the pension scheme. This applies particularly to people about to retire – they must be told what pension they can expect, what conditions affect its payment and what changes (like increases in amount) can automatically be made to it. A non-automatic change (like a discretionary increase you weren't expecting) must be notified too.

● **Death benefit statement** Any adult expecting a benefit following your death, whenever that occurs, must be told how much they can expect and whether or not there are any options for them to choose from. This is an obvious piece of information for the scheme to give your family or others who are dependent on you, but the legal obligation is there on the scheme to contact them, rather than waiting for them to ask.

● **An early leaver statement** You are an 'early leaver' if you change your job or are made redundant. When you hand in your notice, or are given notice, the scheme must give you automatically a statement of your rights from the scheme. This will show if you can take out any of your contributions. If not it will detail what your preserved pension is. It will also explain how you can transfer it to another scheme in your next job or to an insurance contract in your own name. If you don't transfer, but leave your pension rights behind for collection at retirement, you still count as a member of the scheme with rights to information about it.

● **A transfer-out scheme** You have the right to ask, though not more than once a year, for a valuation of your pension rights. This means the value your scheme puts on the rights built up so far if you were to leave either the firm or the scheme, and transfer to another scheme. You might see this as a smart way of measuring the steady growth of your stake in the scheme in cash terms. Unfortunately, however, you could be misled. Your pension rights grow steadily, as you notch up another year's membership on a higher pay figure. But investment conditions change quite independently of the growth. This means that a current valuation of your rights could fluctuate alarmingly, even though your pension rights themselves are quite unaffected.

● **A transfer-in settlement** Many people who leave pension rights behind in a previous scheme want to know whether it is worthwhile transferring those rights to their new employer's scheme. In this case you can ask your present employer (but not more than once a year) what pension rights you would receive if you arranged for a transfer. You might want to choose the right moment to do so, hoping for the best possible deal. But since the transfer value from your old scheme, and the offer your present scheme makes you in exchange, are both worked out on the same 'fair' basis, the right moment can be hard to judge. It is usually best to take advice from your present scheme's manager over whether a transfer now is likely to be in your best interests. If you are unhappy with the answers, consult an independent pensions consultant.

PERSONAL PENSIONS

The legislation covering personal pensions (whether or not they're used for contracting-out and claiming DHSS rebate payments) includes the automatic right to certain information from those investing your contributions. You also have the right to ask for other information. Armed with all of this, you should be in a position to judge how well your personal investment is being looked after. The government see this as particularly important if you are substituting a contracted-out personal pension for the State earnings-related pensions scheme.

AUTOMATIC INFORMATION

Within 13 weeks of starting your personal pension you have to be given a complete picture of the plan you've taken out. For example, you'll be told about how tax relief on your contribution works; how your investment is turned into pension and tax-free cash when you retire; what part of your contributions is used for administration and paying commission; and how the remaining contributions are going to be invested.

Each year you have to be told how much has been paid into your pension plan; what your investment is currently worth; and how much would go into another pension plan if you choose to transfer your investment.

There are also particular occasions which will prompt your chosen investment institution to give further information. Such eventualities would include you being contracted-in to the State earnings-related pension scheme for any reason, or if you stop paying contributions, or if you die.

INFORMATION YOU NEED TO REQUEST

You, your wife or husband, or anyone entitled to benefit from your pension plan can apply for information about the way it works. In particular you all have the right to information about rights and options which come into force after your death. You can ask questions about where your contributions are invested, and about how they have been performing. You cannot demand this information too frequently however – not more than once a year is the usual frequency laid down in the regulations.

As a valued customer of the insurance company (or whatever institution is responsible for your personal pension), you should always be able to rely on them to be obliging. Whoever sold you your personal pension has a strong interest in seeing that you are satisfied because they know there will nearly always be scope for you – in your own best interests – to increase your contributions as you get older.

Before you ever get to invest in a personal pension, you are protected by regulations coming out of the financial services legislation, which puts many stringent obligations on people who sell investment contracts.

The main requirement is that you have to be given 'product information' about the personal pension they are recommending, unless it is based on a building society or a bank deposit account. This should be given at the time of the recommendation or very soon afterwards and is usually in the brochure. It has to give you such details as:

● How the investment linking works in unit-linked contracts and how the charges deducted from your investment are calculated.
● In with-profits contracts, how bonuses are added to your investment after the institution's shareholders have benefited.
● The income and capital gains tax position.
● What happens if you stop contributing.
● How your investment will stand if you want to transfer it to a different pension plan. This information should include transfer value projections worked out on the first five anniversaries of taking your plan out.

In addition, whenever a projection is made on the potential value of your pension fund at retirement, it must be calculated in line with certain rules. These are laid down by the regulatory organisation responsible for supervising unit trusts and insurance companies. They include warnings about how projections need to be judged in the light of future inflation.

One of the most important rights you have is known as a 'cooling-off' notice. This gives you the right to think again and, if you wish, cancel the plan you've taken out. This notice sets out, among other things, how the independent intermediary you may have consulted gets paid for the work he does for you. By law, you have 14 days in which to cancel and so get back the money you have paid into the plan.

This disclosure requirement for personal pensions is a part of the current investor protection regulations. Apart from giving you information, the salesman must also tell you which organisation he works for. He may work for an insurance company, selling only that company's products. Or he may be an independent intermediary or broker, selling whichever pension plan he believes is right for you. In either case, he is bound by two important principles. The first is 'best advice'. This means that he must recommend the product which he believes will perform best for you.

The second is 'know your customer'. This means he must learn from you all relevant facts about you, your family and your financial circumstances. The aim of investor protection rules is to give you confidence in him and what he tells you.

GLOSSARY

Accrued Pension
The amount of pension which you have earned so far as a member of a pension scheme. It is payable from your retirement date.

Actuarial Report
A statement produced by an actuary showing how the assets of a pension scheme compare with its liabilities. It is usually produced once every three years and also makes recommendations as to what the company should pay into the pension fund over the next three years.

Actuary
Someone who is professionally qualified to evaluate the financial state of a pension scheme and make recommendations as to how much money should be paid in to it to provide the benefits promised.

Added Years
Extra pension provided on top of the normal amount given in a final salary scheme. If you have transferred pension rights from one scheme to another, or if you have been making additional voluntary contributions, you may be entitled to a fixed amount of additional pension. Alternatively, this may be converted into extra years and months and added onto the number of years that you have belonged to a pension scheme to increase your benefits.

Additional Voluntary Contributions (AVCs)
Money which you can pay to a pension scheme in order to obtain extra benefits. You may invest up to 15 per cent of your gross pay each year (including any ordinary contributions

you make to your employer's pension scheme) and receive income tax relief at the highest rate you pay tax. AVC schemes can either be organised by your employer or you can get your own independent (known as free-standing) AVC scheme. Schemes established after 7 April 1987 can only provide extra pension benefits – it is not possible to convert the AVC investment into a tax-free cash sum.

Approved Scheme
The Finance Act 1970 states that if an occupational scheme is to qualify for tax relief it must be approved by the Superannuation Funds Office of the Inland Revenue. An 'exempt approved scheme' is one which has been set up under trust and receives full tax relief. An 'approved scheme' is not set up under trust and does not receive all the tax relief possible. Sometimes people refer to approved schemes when they actually mean exempt approved schemes.

Assets
The investments held by a pension scheme which are used to purchase future benefits.

Assumptions
When an actuary forecasts what will happen to a scheme in the future he or she has to make certain calculated assumptions concerning future financial and economic developments. The most important of these is what will happen to rates of pay and to the rate of return on investments.

Augmentation
A scheme's rules usually allow the trustees to grant benefits in addition to the normal scheme entitlement, either to an individual or a group of individuals. Any increase of benefits in this way must remain within the limits laid down by the Inland Revenue.

Boyd Carpenter Scheme
This is the State scheme which existed from 1961 – 1975.
Although the benefits are low, they have been inflation-
proofed since 1978 and are provided on top of other State
scheme pensions.

Buy-out Plan
See Section 32 Policy or Annuity.

Capital Transfer Tax
Tax paid on money or goods that changed ownership. Most
people only came across this tax when property changed
hands following a death. In 1986 this tax was replaced by the
Inheritance Tax.

Cash Option
The option by which you can exchange some of your
pension for a tax-free lump sum when you retire.

Castle Plan
The name sometimes given to the State earnings-related
pension scheme. Barbara Castle was the minister
responsible for this scheme.

Children's Pension
The pension sometimes payable to your child or children if you
die while still a scheme member or after retirement. The
pension would normally be paid until the youngest child
reaches a certain age (usually 18) or finishes full time education.

Commutation
Exchanging part of your pension for a tax-free cash sum. The
maximum amount of money you may receive must not be
more than one-and-a-half times your annual salary at the time
you retire. The pension is usually exchanged at the rate of

£1.00 of pension for £9.00 of cash if you are a man retiring at 65, and £1.00 of pension for £11.00 of cash if you are a woman retiring at 60. If you joined a pension scheme after March 1987, the maximum amount you can receive is £150,000. If you are a member of a cash accumulation scheme, the cash must not exceed three times your pension. If you join a cash accumulation scheme after 1 July 1988, the maximum cash you may take is 25 per cent of the value of your fund. Although most people find this option attractive and decide to exchange pension for cash, you should consider carefully whether this option is right for you.

Contingent Annuity

A pension which does not start to be paid until another event has taken place. For example, a spouse's pension is contingent upon the death of a husband or wife.

Continuation Option

If you leave your pension scheme your life assurance usually stops. Many schemes then allow you the option of taking out your own life assurance cover, without providing medical evidence of good health.

Contracting-out

Opting out of the State earnings-related pension scheme (SERPS). As a result, when you retire, the pension provided by the State will consist only of the basic State pension. There will be no State pension based on your earnings since April 1978. An employer who chooses to contract his or her employees out of the earnings-related pension will pay at least an equivalent pension from his or her own scheme. If you have been contracted-out by your employer, you are paying reduced National Insurance contributions. From 1 July 1988, if you are an employee you can contract out of the State scheme independently of your employer.

Deductive Item

Some pension schemes do not calculate your pension on your total earnings. This is because some employers feel that the State pension adequately covers part of your earnings. The reduction, known as the deductive item, is usually applied when calculating your contributions as well as your pension entitlement. It will not normally be applied when calculating your level of life assurance cover.

Deed

To obtain all the necessary tax reliefs a scheme must be set up under trust. The trust deed is the legal document which establishes the trust. Whenever there are any changes to the scheme (for example, if a new company joins the scheme) a new deed will be required.

Deferred Pensions

When you reach your normal retirement age but decide to delay receiving your pension, your pension will be 'deferred'. The term can also be applied to a 'preserved' pension.

Deficiency / Deficit

If a scheme has liabilities greater than its assets it is said to be in deficit or to have a deficiency.

Department of Health and Social Security (DHSS)

The Government department responsible for administering all social security benefits including the basic pension and State earnings-related pension (SERPS).

Dependant's Option

The right to give up part of your pension when you retire so that your dependants would receive a pension if you died before them.

Dependant's Pension

The pension paid to your dependants (usually your husband or wife and dependent children) if you die.

Discontinuance

The term usually applied if for some reason a scheme stops building up benefits. The benefits which have already built up can either be paid from the scheme at such times as they would normally have been paid, or the scheme can be closed and the benefits due for payment purchased elsewhere – usually with an insurance company.

Dynamism

A name given to increasing pension payments. It can refer to pensions which have not yet started payment, as well as those that have. Other terms include expansion, escalation, inflation proofing and index linking.

Early Leaver

This simply means someone who has changed jobs and left his or her employer's pension scheme.

Early Retirement

You may stop work and start receiving your pension before your normal retirement date. If you do retire early, the pension you receive will usually be lower than that given at your normal retirement date. This is not only because you will have a shorter period of service on which to base your pension, but also because the pension itself is likely to be given for a longer period.

Eligibility

The terms that you must satisfy before you can join a pension scheme. These terms most commonly relate to a minimum age, a minimum length of service and your category of employment. You may be eligible to join for death benefits before you can join for pension benefits.

Equal Access
Eligibility conditions for entry to a scheme must be the same for both men and women. It is permissible to have different upper age limits but only to the extent that male and female retirement ages differ.

Equivalent Pension Benefit
The minimum benefit that must be provided by schemes which decided to contract out of the 1961 – 1975 State graduated pension scheme.

Escalation (Expansion)
Increasing pension payments. In the private sector such increases may be a guaranteed amount (for example, 3 – 5 per cent a year) or they may be at the trustees' discretion. In the public sector, pensions are guaranteed to increase in line with prices.

Evidence of Health
Information about your health which you may be asked to provide before a life assurance company will grant you cover for death benefits. This can involve a medical examination or just the completion of a form. The purpose is to ensure that the insurance company can fix a fair price for what can be a very large amount of cover.

Expansion
See Escalation and Dynamism.

Expression of Wish
On your death the trustees of a pension scheme normally have discretion to decide to whom the death benefits should

be paid. An 'expression of wish' form allows you to tell the trustees to whom you would like the money to be paid. So that this money can be paid free of liability to Inheritance Tax your 'wish' is not binding on the trustees.

Final Pensionable Salary/Earnings

A scheme that bases your pension on a proportion of the salary you are earning at or near retirement, taking into account the number of years you have been a member of the scheme.

Free-standing Additional Voluntary Contributions

Additional voluntary contributions (AVCs; see separate entry) paid for by an individual and independent from his or her employer's scheme. All companies with a pension scheme must offer the facility for paying AVCs. But you can choose to join your own AVC scheme, independently of your employer, with, for example, an insurance company of your choice. From 1 July 1988 you can use this free-standing additional voluntary contribution scheme to contract out of the State earnings-related pension scheme.

Frozen Pension

A pension which is fixed in value and is payable from a future date – usually your normal retirement date.

Graduated Pension

The amount of earnings-related pension built up from 1961 - 1975 under the State graduated scheme.

Guaranteed Minimum Pension (GMP)

This is the amount of pension your scheme must provide if you are contracted out from the State earnings-related pension scheme. The purpose of the GMP is to ensure that you are no worse off as a result of being contracted out than if you had remained a member.

Immediate Annuity
A pension which is bought by a single lump sum which starts payment immediately.

Index Linking
See Inflation-proofing.

Inflation-proofing
Pensions that increase in line with inflation. If your pension is inflation-proofed it will normally be increased in line with prices. It is rare for pensions from schemes in the private sector to be fully inflation-proofed.

Inheritance Tax
This replaced Capital Transfer Tax in 1986 and is paid on the transfer of property following a death. Death benefits paid under discretionary trust by a pension scheme are not usually subject to Inheritance Tax.

Inland Revenue
The government department which deals with all matters concerning taxation.

Insured Scheme
A scheme where an insurance company has agreed to provide a certain level of benefits in return for an agreed level of contributions.

Integration
Some employers make a specific allowance for the pension they will receive from the State when deciding on their pension provision. This is usually done by deciding what overall level of pension employees should receive and then deducting from this the benefits that the State will provide.

Late Retirement
If you carry on working after your normal retirement date you may decide to delay payment of your pension until you actually stop work. If you do this, the pension you will receive when you retire will usually be for an increased amount.

Lower Earnings Limit
This is the level of weekly pay you have to earn before you and your employer pay National Insurance contributions. This figure changes each tax year in line with price increases.

Money Purchase
A type of pension scheme which does not guarantee a level of benefits. Instead, the level of contributions is fixed and at retirement the accumulated value of the fund (which includes contributions, interest and bonuses) is used to buy a pension. Usually the exact amount of pension the fund will buy is not known in advance.

Normal Retirement Date
The date on which payment of your pension will start. In line with the State retirement age, this is normally 65 for men and 60 for women.

Occupational Pensions Board
This is a government body whose main supervisory functions cover, first, those pension schemes which choose to contract out of the State earnings-related scheme and, second, the rights of people who change their jobs.

Options
Choices that you may be offered in connection with your pension benefits. These will normally only be available at a time of change, for example, when you leave the company or retire.

Past Service Pension
If your company starts a pension scheme, your pension will usually be based on the number of years' service given to the company, starting from the date the scheme commenced. However, your employer may decide to make all your employment with the company pensionable. Because of the cost to the employer, this past service pension may be on a reduced rate.

Pension
A regular payment to someone who has retired, or to the dependants of a member of a pension scheme who has died.

Pensionable Earnings/Salary
The earnings upon which the calculation of both pension and contributions is usually based. Pensionable earnings may not always be the same as your total earnings because they may exclude any overtime or bonuses you earn.

Pensionable Service
The length of time you have spent with your employer which qualifies for inclusion when calculating your pension benefits. This is either expressed in whole years or years and months.

Permanent Health Insurance
This provides you with an income should you be unable to work owing to ill health. Benefit is not normally paid immediately you are off work but may be deferred for a period of up to a year. However, during this time you would normally be receiving sick pay from your employer. The amount of money paid varies but is typically 50 per cent of your earnings before you stopped working. Once payment has started it continues until you return to work, retire or die. The payments can cover the cost of maintaining pension and death benefits.

Personal Pensions

Prior to 1 July 1988 this term referred to a non-employer sponsored pension taken out with an insurance company by someone who was self-employed or in non-pensionable employment. These schemes are often referred to as S226 schemes. From 1 July 1988, a new kind of personal pension is being introduced. Like the existing personal pensions they are taken out by individuals, but employees will be able to use them for contracting-out of the State earnings-related scheme and will be allowed to have contributions from their employer invested in them. Personal pensions will be able to receive transfer values for benefits earned in previous pensionable employment and will be completely portable.

Preservation

If you leave your pension scheme and have been a member for at least two years, your scheme must provide you with a pension when you retire. You are entitled to transfer the cash value of this preserved pension to another employer's scheme or to an individual insurance policy.

Prolonged Disability Scheme

See Permanent Health Insurance.

Protected Rights

From 6 April 1988 it has been possible to contract-out of the State earnings-related pension scheme using a personal pension or money purchase scheme. Any such scheme must keep a separate record of the DHSS rebate payments invested in it, since these are subject to certain rules due to being substituted for the State pension.

Purchased Life Annuity

This is a pension that someone can buy with their own money as opposed to a pension which is purchased by a pension scheme. The main difference between the two types of pension is that the tax treatments are more generous for a purchased life annuity than they are for an annuity purchased by a pension scheme.

Refund
The return of any contributions that you may have paid into your pension scheme if you leave your employer after being a member of the scheme for two years. If a refund is payable a 10 per cent reduction will be made for tax and you may have to pay to be brought back into the State earnings-related scheme if you were contracted out. If you should die before retirement as a current member of a pension scheme, a refund of your contributions is usually paid to your estate.

Revaluation
This is a means of ensuring that the value of a fixed amount of money does not lose its purchasing power. It applies particularly to preserved pensions for early leavers.

Salary Sacrifice
Some schemes allow their members to give up part of their salary in return for increased pension benefits. Salary sacrifice options are particularly attractive to higher rate tax payers.

Section 32 Policy or Annuity
If you leave a pension scheme you can usually transfer the cash value of the benefits you have earned to a pension plan operated by an insurance company of your own choice. The insurance company will then provide you with whatever benefits can be bought with the value of the policy (also known as a buy-out policy) when you come to retire.

Self-administered Scheme
A scheme run by an employer independently of an insurance company.

State Earnings-related Pension Scheme
This scheme began in 1978 and produces pensions which are linked to number of years of contribution and amount of earning during those years. Its pensions are being cut back substantially for people retiring after the end of the century.

State Pension Age
The age at which payment of the State pension begins. This is 65 for men and 60 for women.

Superannuation
Another word for pension.

Superannuation Funds Office
A department of the Inland Revenue responsible for supervising pension schemes and getting approval in order for them to qualify for tax reliefs.

Surplus
Where a scheme's assets exceed its liabilities the scheme is said to be in surplus.

Tax Relief
Schemes which receive full Inland Revenue approval are eligible for considerable tax advantages. These include income tax relief on employees' contributions at the highest rate of tax and a tax-free lump sum at retirement. In addition, any money invested in a pension fund is not liable to Income Tax or Capital Gains Tax while employer's contributions are an allowed expense against Corporation Tax.

Transferability
Your right to transfer some pension rights from one scheme to another. This can either be to another employer-sponsored scheme, an S32 annuity or (from 1 July 1988) to a personal pension plan.

Transfer Club
An arrangement set up between a group of pension schemes by which employees who transfer between their pension schemes will receive favourable treatment. The best known transfer club mainly comprises public sector schemes.

Transfer Value
A lump sum, representing the cash value of the benefits you have earned with one employer, is paid from one pension scheme to another. This transfers the liability for your pension benefits for this period from one fund to another. Partial transfer values may have to be paid on occasion.

Trivial Pension
An amount of pension which the Inland Revenue regards as so small it can be exchanged in full for cash. From 1 January 1988, the maximum amount of pension which can be treated in this way is £104.00 per annum.

Trustees
A group of people who ultimately are responsible for all aspects of a pension scheme. The powers and responsibilities of trustees are laid down in the trust deed.

Unit Linked Scheme
A scheme where the level of benefits provided at retirement depends partly or entirely on investment performance.

Upper Earnings Limit
The level of earnings above which you do not have to pay National Insurance contributions. (This limit does not apply to employers.) The State earnings-related scheme does not provide any pension on earnings above this level.

Valuation
The assessment, by actuary, of a scheme's financial status, taking into account its assets and liabilities.

Vested Right
The right to receive a pension even if you have left the scheme before retirement age.

Waiting Period
The length of time you have to wait before you become eligible to join your employer's scheme for pension or death benefits.

Widow's Pension
A pension payable to a widow on the death of her husband, on death, before or after retirement.

Widower's Pension
A pension payable to a widower on the death of his wife, before or after retirement.

Winding Up
If a scheme ceases to exist the scheme's assets have to be disposed of. This can be done by purchasing benefits from another body, usually an insurance company. The scheme would then cease to exist and the scheme members would receive their benefits from the insurance company.

Withdrawal Option

A statement outlining the options available to you with regard to your pension, should you leave your employment before retirement age. The options may include a refund, a preserved pension or a transfer value.

With-profit

A policy which shares in any profits declared by an insurance company. This can be reflected either by reduced premiums or through bonuses which increase the level of benefits payable.

USEFUL ADDRESSES

**Company Pensions
Information Centre**
7 Old Park Lane
London W1Y 3LJ
Tel: 01 493 4757
*CPIC gives general
information about
occupational pensions,
supplying speakers for
seminars and lectures,
and publishing simple
booklets.*

**The National Association
of Pension Funds**
12/18 Grosvenor Gardens
London SW1W 0DH
Tel: 01 730 0585
*The NAPF is the
representative body for all
kinds of employer-
sponsored schemes and is
active in putting their views
to politicians and official
pensions bodies.*

**The Pensions
Management Institute**
124 Middlesex Street
London E1 7HY
Tel: 01 247 1452
*The Institute is concerned
with education, leading to
a professional qualification,
for people working in the
many aspects of pension
plans of all kinds.*

**The Society of Pension
Consultants**
Ludgate House
Ludgate Circus
London EC4A 2AB
Tel: 01 353 1688
*The Society represents
the organisations which
give advice to employers
and individuals about
pension planning and
legislative developments.*

**The British Insurance
Brokers' Association**
14 Bevis Marks
London EC3A 7NT
Tel: 01 623 9043
*The Association
represents insurance
brokers and is
responsible for setting
standards of behaviour
towards members of
the public.*

The Association of British Insurers
Aldermary House
10/15 Queen Street
London EC4N 1TT
Tel: 01 248 4477
The Association's life insurance council is involved in representing insurance company views to the government on subjects which include pensions, and in raising public awareness.

Institute of Actuaries
Staple Inn Hall
High Holborn
London WC1V 7QJ
Tel: 01 242 0106
Faculty of Actuaries in Scotland
23 St Andrews Square
Edinburgh EH2 1AQ
Tel: 031 557 1575
These are the professional bodies for actuaries in the UK.

The Association of Consulting Actuaries
47/49 London Road
Reigate
Surrey RH2 9PQ
Tel: 07372 41144
The Association represents actuaries who are in full time professional practice.

Joint Office of Superannuation Funds Office and Occupational Pensions Board
Lynwood Road
Thames Ditton
Surrey KT20 0DP
Tel: 01 398 4242
This is the combined headquarters of the Superannuation Funds Office (part of the Inland Revenue) and the Occupational Pensions Board, which between them supervise and administer tax and other legislation for pension plans of every kind.